GEORGE BRETT:
A ROYAL HERO

SPORTS PUBLISHING INC.
www.SportsPublishingInc.com

Coordinating Editor: Mark Zeligman
Developmental Editors: Victoria J. Parrillo and Joseph J. Bannon, Jr.
Director of Production: Susan M. McKinney
Book design, project manager: Jennifer L. Polson
Dustjacket, photo section design: Julie L. Denzer
Photo Editor: Greg Booker
Proofreader: David Hamburg

ISBN: 1-58261-034-7
Library of Congress Number: 99-62253

Printed in the United States.

SPORTS PUBLISHING INC.
www.SportsPublishingInc.com

Acknowledgments

Throughout George Brett's incredible career, *The Kansas City Star* gave Brett's fans a front row seat for every historic milestone. Bringing these achievements to life in the pages of the *Star* requires the hard work and dedication of many people at the paper. Among those who were instrumental in getting this project off the ground were Monroe Dodd and Doug Weaver, who supported us from beginning to end. I would also like to thank our Coordinating Editor, Mark Zeligman, for his guidance and expertise on the career of George Brett, and Joe Posnanski for writing the featured tribute essay and many other contributions throughout the book.

Others at the paper whose assistance on this project was invaluable were photographers Keith Myers, Jim McTaggart, Fred Blocher, and Steve Gonzalez. I would also like to acknowledge Greg Booker, Derek Donovan, Jo Ann Groves, Faith Allen, and Jennifer Davis for all their support during our time at the paper. Finally, we are grateful to copy editors Paul Hanson and Chris Carter for their editing assistance.

Space limitations preclude me from thanking each writer and photographer whose work appears in this book. However, whenever possible, I have preserved the writers' bylines and the photographers' credits to ensure proper attribution for their work.

And finally, I am grateful for all the support and hard work of those at Sports Publishing Inc. who worked tirelessly on this project. Special thanks go to Joseph Bannon, Jr. for his guidance and patience with me throughout this project. I would also like to recognize Jennifer Polson, Susan McKinney, Julie Denzer, Mike Pearson, Joanna Wright, David Hamburg, Scot Muncaster, and Claudia Mitroi for all of their hard work.

Victoria J. Parrillo
Developmental Editor

contents

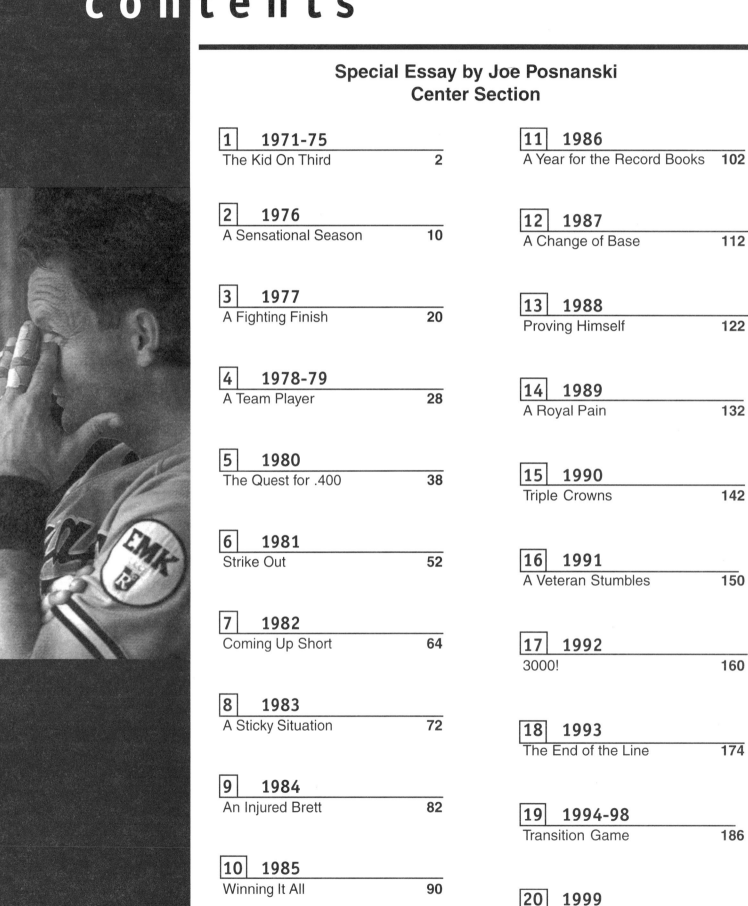

Special Essay by Joe Posnanski
Center Section

You take a kid like Brett and you figure you've got your third baseman for the next 10 or 15 years. He'll be the best in the game.

—Royals manager Jack McKeon

The Kid on Third

Coming out of El Segundo (Calif.) High School in 1971, George Brett was best known to baseball scouts as Ken Brett's younger brother. While his name was familiar, it was George's talent that made him the Royals' second pick in the 1971 baseball draft. Originally scouted as a strong-armed shortstop with good hands and a good bat, the 18-year-old Brett was shifted to third base when he reported to the Royals' minor-league club in Billings, Mont.

Quickly rising through the Royals' farm system, Brett made his major-league debut as a late-season call-up in 1973. While not spectacular, Brett showed enough promise that he returned to the majors for good after only 16 games of the 1974 minor-league season.

As Brett's star continued to rise at the major-league level—he batted .282 in 1974 and .308 in 1975—comparisons to his older brother began to fade, and the name Brooks Robinson was heard more often in conversations about Brett. After he was selected as the Royals' top player for the 1975 season, George was poised to move into the class of baseball's elite.

A young George Brett runs the bases at El Segundo High School in California. Brett played catcher for three years in high school before he was moved to shortstop in his senior year.

june 9, 1971

by Del Black

Tradition Favors Royals in Choice of Prep Star

Tradition appears to be on the Royals' side in their selection of Roy Branch as their first choice in the major-league baseball draft. And as Lou Gorman, Royals' director of scouting, and 10 members of his staff believe, this young athlete has more than tradition upon which to rely.

Branch is a 17-year-old right-handed pitcher from Beaumont High School in St. Louis. Ten Beaumont graduates have made it to the major leagues. They are: Bud Blattner, Chuck Diering, Bobby Hofman, Jack Maguire, Jim Goodwin, Roy Sievers, Bob Wiesler, Lloyd Merritt, Lee Thomas and Bob Miller. Blattner, of course, is an announcer for the Royals.

Along the managerial trail, Earl Weaver of the Baltimore Orioles is a product of Beaumont.

Gorman and 10 Royals' scouts laid the groundwork for the first-round selection of Branch, a 5-11, 180-pound right-handed pitcher. He's the player they wanted and he was available when the Royals drafted fifth yesterday in the first round of the regular phase of the draft in New York.

Branch, who also plays third base and carries a .340 batting average, was an all-Metro quarterback in St. Louis last year, the first time a Negro has been chosen the top quarterback in the city. Selection as all-district Back of the Year and honorable mention for Missouri All-State also belong to Branch, who has received 16 football and 10 collegiate baseball scholarship offers.

Kansas City pegged 10 other players yesterday during the first of two days of drafting.

George Brett, brother of pitcher Ken Brett of the Boston Red Sox, was the Royals' second choice. An 18-year-old shortstop from El Segundo (Calif.) High School, young Brett bats left-handed, stands 6 feet and weighs 160. "He has good hands and a good bat," Gorman says. "We believe he will be a good line-drive hitter with power."

George Brett plays shortstop for his El Segundo High School baseball team.

1971–1975

by Sid Bordman

Royals See Gold Already in Free-Agent Draft

So far the Royals have landed 10 of their first 12 selections in the June free-agent draft. And if the 1973 catch is anything like the one in 1971, the farm system will be nurturing at least two or three new prime major-league prospects.

"The '71 draft was a good one for us," said Lou Gorman, the enthusiastic director of Kansas City's minor leagues and scouting operations. "George Brett and Tom Poquette, our Nos. 2 and 4 picks, already are with Omaha and are outstanding prospects."

Brett, a left-handed-hitting third baseman who became 20 years old last month, is swatting away at a .293 average and has collected five home runs and 40 runs batted in for the AAA farm club. Poquette, also 20, is playing right field.

"These are our top two, the two closest to being up here. We're not the only club that thinks Brett and Poquette are almost ready. We haven't talked to a club about trading in the last two or three weeks that hasn't asked for Brett or Poquette."

Jack McKeon, the Royals' manager, agrees with Gorman on his evaluation of Brett and Poquette, a left-handed hitter.

"Yeah," he remarked. "I got a pretty good look at both of them in spring training. Poquette doesn't do anything flashy but he gets the things done. Brett has the tools to play up here, too."

> I got a pretty good look at both of them in spring training . . . Brett has the tools to play up here, too.
> —Lou Gorman, director of Kansas City's minor leagues

Brett's Minor League STATS

YEAR	CLUB	AVG.	G	AB	R	H	2B	3B	HR	RBI	BB	SO	SB
1971	Billings	.291	68	258	44	75	8	5	5	44	32	38	3
1972	San Jose	.274	117	431	66	118	13	5	10	68	53	53	2
1973	Omaha	.284	117	405	66	115	16	4	8	64	48	45	3
1974	Omaha	.266	16	64	9	17	2	0	2	14	6	1	1

by Gib Twyman

Swinging Royals Sweep into First

Brett Makes Debut

CHICAGO—There were no rahs. Nary a sis, boom or a bah. Not so much as one "No. 1" shouted in the dressing room. There are too many games left for that.

The Royals climbed to the summit by clawing their way 14 games over the .500 mark at 62-48 with their fifth straight victory in their last 15 games, 20th in their last 28. The Athletics succumbed to the assault on their stranglehold of first by dipping to 60-48 with a .566 percentage, eight points back of the Royals.

But Fran Healy let them waste nothing in the ninth. Lou Piniella laced a single to left and moved to second as Ed Kirkpatrick laid down a perfect sacrifice bunt. George Brett, playing his first major-league game, moved Lou to third with a grounder to first and then Healy came through with his single to center.

It was a textbook inning for acquiring runs of any kind, especially insurance runs. The kind you might expect, really, of a first-place team.

Royals Win as Brett Gets First Home Run

May 9, 1974
By Gib Twyman

ARLINGTON, Texas—Kansas City notched its third straight victory as it began a nine-game road trip by stretching Texas' losing streak to four, the longest of the season for the Western Division-leading Rangers.

Hal McRae gave the Royals a 1-0 lead in the third inning, singling home Amos Otis from second with one out. Then George Brett, who had gone 3-for-4 in the victory over New York Sunday, hit his first major-league homer in the seventh, a 390-foot drive over the right-field fence that gave Kansas City a 2-0 advantage.

1971–1975

by Sid Bordman

Royals' Rookie Keeps Raising His Sights

George Brett is raising his sights.

At the All-Star game break, the Royals' rookie third baseman was hitting .242.

"If I can get up to .260, I figure it will be a pretty fair year," he remarked then.

"Now I'm thinking about .285," said the young Californian yesterday, solving Ferguson Jenkins for three hits in four trips in Texas. "If I can get a couple of hits a game the rest of the way I can do it. Say I get 18 hits in the last nine games. That'll do it. It may sound like a lot of hits, but when you're hot you're confident."

Brett, one of the leading candidates for the American League Rookie of the Year award, has been on a swatting tear and has raised his average 36 percentage points to .277 with 57-for-170 during the last 43 games.

In Kansas City's 2-out-of-3 sacking of the Rangers over the weekend Brett went 5-for-12, driving in five runs.

Brett, who has three homers to go with his 42 runs batted in, says he is not satisfied with his glove work even though he is developing a reputation as a solid third baseman.

"Too many errors on routine plays, just stupid things on my part," he said.

Staff photo, Kansas City Star

George Brett is congratulated by teammate Hal McRae at home plate. Brett was a leading candidate for the AL Rookie of the Year award, but was edged out by first baseman Mike Hargrove of Texas.

1971–1975

july 15, 1975

by Sid **Bordman**

Brett Looking a Lot Like Uncrowned All-Star

As usual, the All-Star ballot is vulnerable to criticism.

Neither Dave Chalk of California nor George Brett of the Royals is among the eight third basemen on the American League list.

With Brooks Robinson of Baltimore struggling with the bat and Don Money of Milwaukee slowed by an injury, Brett has moved near the head of the class of major league third basemen.

Because of the relatively small population here, Brett's chances of landing an All-Star berth as a write-in candidate are nil.

But the situation doesn't disturb Kansas City's 22-year-old third baseman.

"The other guys on the ballot have been around for a long time," said Brett, whose .286 batting average (through last Friday) trailed only Chalk's .305 among AL third basemen. "Some of these guys still are on it. When I'm 30, maybe my name still will be on it. The All-Stars are picked by the fans, not the players or managers. The fans have a right to do what they wish."

Brett Named Royals' Top Player

by Del Black
December 3, 1975

That kid at third base for the Royals has another reason to remember his first complete major-league season.

George Brett was named the Royals' Player of the Year today.

"I am really thrilled," he said. "It gives me a great deal of satisfaction, especially because it's a Kansas City award. I was pretty happy with my performance, but now the important thing is to be consistent. My main objective is to cut down on my throwing errors."

Consistency was the trademark of Brett's labors last season, a tour of duty in which he led the American League with 195 hits, was sixth with a .308 batting average and set the pace with 13 triples. His 89 runs batted in were second only to John Mayberry (109) among Royals.

1971–1975

If I had to pick the guy who would be the best third baseman in the league for the next 10 years, I'd have to say George Brett.

—Brooks Robinson, Orioles third baseman

A Sensational Season

At only 23 years young, George Brett put together an All-Star season in 1976 that earned him the American League batting title and made him a superstar. With his face on the cover of national magazines, and TV cameras showing his famous swing to millions, Brett was everywhere.

In one remarkable stretch early in the season, Brett accomplished a feat that no other ballplayer had ever done before—he had six straight three-hit games. Brett's impressive play landed him on his first American League All-Star team—winning the fans' vote as the starting third baseman in a landslide.

Brett's magnificent 1976 season closed with controversy and agony. The controversy arose when Brett edged teammate Hal McRae for the American League batting title on the final day of the season. Needing a hit in his last at-bat, Brett looped a routine fly ball to short left field. When the Twins left fielder misplayed the ball into an inside-the-park home run, hints of racism against the Twins and favoritism toward Brett were raised, but never substantiated. And the agony came soon after, when with one quick, agonizing flick of the bat, the Yankees' Chris Chambliss ended the Royals' season.

by Steve Marantz

Brett Riding High on Magic Carpet of Success

It's all happening so fast for George Brett, the kid on third. His life crackles like an old-fashioned movie reel; the time frame is jerky, the vision blurred.

At the age of 23 he is a celebrity. His face smiles boyishly up from a million American coffee tables, his image and voice are beamed to the nation.

Fame is deluging Brett. He is fresh grist for the vast American publicity mill and he is being served up, base hit by base hit. His fame is coming in a torrent, harder and faster than Brett would have thought possible.

"I pretty much woke up one morning and there it was, all of a sudden," he says, amazed.

His life has a magic carpet quality. There he is, George Brett, All-Star third baseman, the ladies' choice, and eternal boy of summer with his hat on crooked and a hole in each sock.

At 21, he was the Royals' starting third baseman and already they compared him to Brooks Robinson. At 22, he led the American league in base hits and they said Robinson in his prime could never have carried Brett's bat.

This season no one can carry his bat. In early May he made three hits a game in six consecutive games, a feat thought to be a major-league record. Brett won by a landslide in the All-Star voting. Through last night, Brett led the major leagues with a .349 average and 155 hits.

1976 Associated Press
ALL-STAR Baseball Team

Position	Player	Avg.	HRs	RBI
1B	Rod Carew, Minn.	.331	9	90
2B	Joe Morgan, Cin.	.320	21	111
SS	Dave Concepcion, Cin.	.281	9	69
3B	George Brett, KC	.333	7	67
OF	George Foster, Cin.	.306	29	121
OF	Mickey Rivers, NYY	.312	8	67
OF	Ken Griffey, Cin.	.336	6	74
C	Thurman Munson, NYY	.302	17	105
Pitcher		**W**	**L**	**ERA**
R	Jim Palmer, Balt.	22	13	2.51
L	Randy Jones, SD	22	14	2.74

1976

by Steve Marantz

Brett Was Sure He Could Beat LaRoche

In one mad, fitful dash last night, George Brett executed one of baseball's most daring and infrequent plays. His 10th-inning steal of home plate provided the Royals with a 4-3 victory over Cleveland at Royals Stadium and for an instant revived one of baseball's lost arts.

For Brett it was a major-league first and for the Royals it was the second such theft this season, Dave Nelson having made one August 8 in Chicago.

"It is the most exciting play in baseball," said Nelson, who happened to be at bat last night when Brett broke for home. Nelson reacted coolly to the sight of Brett charging toward him. With two out and the count at one strike and one ball, Nelson held his swing and made room in the batter's box for Brett's arrival.

Pitcher Dave LaRoche's pitch was low and outside and by the time catcher Rick Cerone gloved it, Brett had completed his journey. LaRoche, a slow-moving left-handed pitcher, stared disconsolately at the home plate scene. Most of the Cleveland players stood still for a few seconds before starting slowly toward their dugout. The Royals mobbed their young hero and pummeled him with delight.

"I've done it on the front end of a double steal before," said Brett. "Never like that."

Before going to the plate in the 10th inning, Brett was convinced he could steal home plate off LaRoche if the opportunity arose. He and Manager Whitey Herzog had agreed that LaRoche's delivery allowed enough time for the steal if the runner committed himself early and quickly to it. As it happened Brett singled, stole second base and advanced to third on the catcher's throwing error.

Nelson came to bat and Brett turned to Chuck Hiller, his third base coach, after the first pitch. Hiller agreed that the time was almost ripe and Brett waited for another pitch before breaking on the third.

"If I hadn't made it, I never would have heard the end of it," Brett said, adding with a laugh. "Now they'll never hear the end of it.

"I was looking at the scoreboard. I knew Oakland was ahead, 5-4, and I thought how much we needed to win," said Brett. "I said to Chuck, 'God, I think I can make it. Look how slow his wind-up was.' Chuck said, 'OK, go if you want to but be safe. Don't be out.'

"I got an extra fat lead," Brett recalled. "As soon as he started into his motion I went down. It was a long way.

"I knew George had an 80 to 90 percent chance of making it from watching that pitcher," said Hiller. "George isn't the fastest guy in the world but he's aggressive. He's got the competitive spirit in him."

1976

by Sid Bordman

Brett's Clinching Hit Draws Rage Reviews

Whether it was a conspiracy or not, George Brett captured the American League batting championship on a hit doused with suspicion.

The dramatic finish to the 1976 batting race was an unfortunate twist to a stirring duel by Brett and Hal McRae, both of whom were feeling the heat of Rod Carew until the fifth inning of yesterday's series finale between the Royals and Minnesota.

After Brett's fly ball fell in front of Steve Brye in left field and became an inside-the-park home run in the ninth, McRae grounded to shortstop Luis Gomez for the second out.

With the Twins in front, 5-3, and no extra innings in sight, Brett's average stopped at .333333 and McRae's at .3320682.

As McRae turned to his right and toward the dugout after his final chance to pass Brett, he turned to the Minnesota dugout and showed his disgust. McRae's manifestation of his emotions was directed at Gene Mauch, Minnesota manager.

Mauch bolted from the dugout toward the Royals' side of the field. The umpires and others on both clubs finally contained Mauch.

McRae, who started the final day of the season with less than a percentage point edge over both Brett and Carew, fought back the tears as he took on the inevitable task of talking to reporters.

"Too bad it was like that," McRae said. "I just hope that everybody knows why I lost. I hope that I won't have to explain what happened at home.

"I was glad to see George win, but I'm sorry to see it happen that way. If he got a clean hit, if he just gets a decent hit I wouldn't have been so disappointed. That I lost isn't the big thing. The way I lost is."

McRae, a black, did not mention the word "race." But he did not hide the fact that he felt there were undercurrents.

"This is America and not that much has changed," McRae said. "Too bad in 1976 things are still like that.

"I was surprised that they deliberately let the ball drop in for George. The guy out there played it so well that he played it into a home run. I saw him come in, go back, come in and stop."

Mauch, visibly upset over McRae's accusation, said that he imagined that there was some animosity on his club toward the aggressive Royals' slugger. "Hal played tough on our club. But that's the way you're supposed to play. I played aggressively all my life. I would never complain about somebody else.

"This thing hurts me more than anything that has ever happened in my 35 years in baseball. I wouldn't do anything to hurt the game.

"I trust Steve Brye implicitly, and if I felt that he did something dishonest, I'd do everything I could to run him out of the game."

1976

Before flying home to Bradenton, Fla., for a couple of days of rest before starting workouts for the play-offs against the Yankees, McRae looked ahead.

"I'm not going to let this affect me in the playoffs or anytime," he pointed out. "I shouldn't have let the race get so close. Next year I just have to go out and get a big lead."

Brett, who also led the league with 14 triples and tied for the lead in doubles with 34, rang up his 29th three-hit game and seventh against the Twins this season. He agreed with McRae on his final hit.

"I thought Brye let the ball drop in—but I'm not sure. He was coming hard. I just wish I had hit a line drive and knocked off somebody's glove.

"Really, I wish the thing could have ended in a tie. I got a present from the Twins."

Brett, who finished with 215 hits to set the AL pace in that category, too, wanted to win the hitting crown.

"Pretty bad when you win the batting title and still feel awful. Mac and I like to see each other do good. When he's going good I'm happy. I shook his hand after the first hits. We were having fun during the game. Everybody wants to win as many honors as possible."

When asked if he had talked with McRae, Brett said, "No."

"Right now I think it's best that I don't talk to him. We'll get together Wednesday when we work out. I can't go up to him and say, 'Nice try.'"

Whitey Herzog, the Royals' manager, shook his head in disbelief.

"Hell of a battle," he grimaced. "As far as I'm concerned, both of these guys are champions."

It was the first time since 1961 that two teammates finished back-to-back for the hitting crown. The controversy of the 1976 AL hitting race will not easily be forgotten.

Staff photo, Kansas City Star

George Brett is honored as the 1976 batting champion.

october 10, 1976

by Mike DeArmond

Brett Abhorred Mouth That Roared

In his wildest dreams, George Brett couldn't have concocted more of a nightmare than the one he lived through yesterday.

The Royals' third baseman will be able to forget his two first-inning errors, costly wild throws that handed the New York Yankees two runs and sent them winging to a 4-1 victory in the first game of the American League playoffs at Royals Stadium.

Billy Martin and the obscenities he heaped on Brett will not soon fade into Never-Never land, however.

"Your brother's an (obscenity), your brother's a (another obscenity) . . . every time I came to bat," Brett said, quoting the New York manager. "I couldn't hear him out in the field; 41,077 other people were on me in the first inning.

"That's really high-class, really a tribute to baseball. If you put a tape recorder on his comments during the game, it would be one blank tape. He was bad-mouthing my brother to get on me because either he was lying or my brother was lying to me. And I don't think my brother was lying."

Brett has been outspoken over what he terms the Yankees' shoddy treatment of his brother, Ken, a pitcher traded to the White Sox only two days after Martin had told him that he would not be swapped.

This is the way George tells it: "After Larry (Gura, the Royals' starting and losing pitcher yesterday) was traded, my brother went to him (Martin) and said, 'I guess I'm next.' Martin said, 'No, I'm going to keep you with me.' Two days later he was gone."

Told what Brett had to say after the game, Martin said, "The players were on him, that's all."

Brett said Martin's was the only voice he heard dishing out four-letter words.

"George Brett had no right making that comment. Personally, I like the guy. He's a great player."

Brett felt like anything but a great player yesterday—despite going 3-for-4 at the plate. But, no, he didn't feel he had lost the game with his first-inning errors—the first a high throw past John Mayberry at first after Mickey Rivers had beaten out a bouncer to third and the second a low throw that skipped past Mayberry in a bases-loaded situation, letting in two runs, after Brett had stepped on third for a force.

Brett, playing in his first playoff game, as were so many of the Royals, admitted he was nervous.

"Nervous? The time I was most nervous all day was when they were making the introductions, going out onto the field.

"I don't think I choked," Brett said with a level stare. "I was nervous. I'm not afraid to admit it. But I don't think I choked.

"What's done is done," he said. "If I sit home and pout about it or feel sorry for myself, I'll keep making errors."

1976

by Del Black

Ninth-Inning Drama Sinks Royals, 7-6

NEW YORK—The home run was a double-edged sword for the Royals last night. They lived by it and died by it.

Chris Chambliss drilled Mark Littell's first pitch in the bottom of the ninth inning into the right-center field bleachers to give the New York Yankees a 7-6 victory and the American League championship.

An inning earlier, George Brett's three-run homer rocketed the Royals into a 6-6 deadlock. And back in the first inning, John Mayberry's one-run round-tripper provided Kansas City with a fast start, one that Dennis Leonard, the first of five pitchers, couldn't maintain.

After wiping out the 2-0 deficit in their half of the first, the Yankees overcame a 3-2 Royals' advantage with two tallies in the third inning and climbed to a 6-3 bulge in the sixth, the final run coming on a throwing error by Brett.

Ed Figueroa, the Yankee starter, settled down after yielding three runs on four hits in the opening two innings and permitted only three singles until the eighth.

After being tagged for a leadoff single in the eighth, Figueroa was replaced by southpaw Grant Jackson.

Another Kansas City single preceded Brett's distant shot that tied the game.

Chambliss, who had three hits and as many runs batted in last night, answered the challenge by hammering a Littell fastball for his 11th of the series.

Ironically, Chambliss never touched third and he didn't touch home plate as pandemonium engulfed Yankee Stadium.

By the time the burly first baseman had started his home run trot, thousands among the record Yankee Stadium turnout of 56,821 had stormed the field.

Chambliss might have touched second base, but when he reached third, the base had been removed. He had no chance of completing the trek to the plate, being devoured by the fans somewhere near the batter's box.

"I touched where I thought third base should be," Chambliss said.

Later it was reported that police escorted Chambliss to the field and he officially touched the plate.

Manager Whitey Herzog of the Royals was angered by the turn of events, which

> **Chambliss might have touched second base, but when he reached third, the base had been removed. He had no chance of completing the trek to the plate, being devoured by the fans somewhere near the batter's box.**

The Royals' first trip to the playoffs ended with the Yankees celebrating a series-winning homer by Chris Chambliss.

included a delay before Littell's disastrous pitch because bottles and debris were being thrown onto the field.

Later, Herzog offered congratulations to the Yankees, adding: "They won't be embarrassed by Cincinnati in the World Series."

Leonard failed to get an out in the first inning and was replaced by Paul Splittorff, whose three bases on balls and three hits cost him two runs in the $3 \frac{2}{3}$ innings he toiled. Marty Pattin worked a third of an inning without incident, giving way to Andy Hassler, who also had trouble finding the plate—walking three—and giving up two hits and a pair of runs in $2 \frac{1}{3}$ frames.

Mayberry's homer, to the 350-foot mark in right field, with Brett on base after he doubled, was the big first baseman's first since August 14 when he connected off Dave Lemanczyk of Detroit at Royals Stadium. It gave Kansas City a 2-0 first-inning lead.

Brett's game-tying blast came after consecutive singles by Al Cowens and pinch-hitter Jim Wohlford.

Cowens opened the eighth with a line drive to left. Grant Jackson, a left-hander, replaced Figueroa.

With Tom Poquette, a left-handed batter, slated to hit, Wohlford grabbed a bat and looped a single to center. Then came Brett's homer, high and deep into the right-field seats.

by The Kansas City Star

Brett Named Top Player

George Brett, a dominant force in American League hitting departments throughout a sensational 1976 season, added another significant statistic today when he became the first Royal to win two straight Kansas City Player of the Year awards.

Brett led the league and set Royal records with a .333 average and 215 hits. He led the league in total bases (298), triples (14) and at-bats (645). He was tied for second in doubles (34) and games played (159) and finished fourth in runs (93) and sixth in slugging percentage (.461).

His 215 hits represented the fourth-highest American League total in the last 35 seasons as he became the first player in 21 years of Kansas City major-league baseball to break the 200-hit barrier.

Perhaps most amazing was Brett's consistency. He reeled off 29 games with three or more hits, including five four-hit games and one five-hit.

In one spectacular string, George re-corded what is believed to be a major-league record with six consecutive three-hit games from May 8-13 when he went 18-for-26 (.692). He also put together a span of 111 straight games from July 1-30 without striking out.

He has not gone more than three games without a hit in the last two years and now owns a .306 batting average for three big-league seasons.

Brett's brilliant play was only one of the reasons the Royals won the American League West Division title, but he also was at his best in the pressure-packed championship playoff series against New York. Before Kansas City bowed out in the fifth and final game, Brett had hit .444 (8-for-18) with a double, triple, homer, four runs and team-high five RBIs.

It will be awhile before anyone forgets that homer—a dramatic three-run shot in the eighth that forged a 6-6 tie before Chris Chambliss won it for the Yankees with his own dramatic homer in the bottom of the ninth of the deciding game.

1976

I'm an aggressive player. I'll do anything to win.
—George Brett

A Fighting Finish

Contract negotiations filled the days between the 1976 and 1977 seasons. After signing a 5-year, 1.5 million-dollar contract, Brett was "on the map" as a respected ballplayer.

Secure in his future with the Royals, Brett resumed his aggressive play. Along with this aggressive style, however, came the injuries. He was sidelined for a week by an elbow injury suffered in a fight with the Texas Rangers, and the injury hampered his play into July. Despite the injury, he was selected to the American League All-Star team for the second straight time of his career. Brett also found time off the field to repay baseball's "kissing bandit" with a much-publicized visit to her place of work.

Brett left his sense of humor behind once he entered the post- season. In game five of the AL playoffs, he was the center of a bench-clearing brawl with Graig Nettles and the New York Yankees, who eventually won the game and the series. Once again, the Royals hit the Yankee "wall" and were unable to move on to their first World Series.

by The Kansas City Star

Brett to Be Out Perhaps a Week

We may be able to use him as a designated hitter, but we're hesitant to because we don't want him to aggravate the injury.

—Royals manager Whitey Herzog

T hird baseman George Brett of the Royals might be sidelined for a week with the elbow injury he suffered last Saturday night in a fight with the Texas Rangers.

"We'll take it day to day and see what happens," said Manager Whitey Herzog yesterday after Brett reported to Royals Stadium with his right elbow still too sore to play. "We may be able to use him as a designated hitter, but we're hesitant to because we don't want him to aggravate the injury."

Brett, the American League's batting champion last season, is now hitting .327. X-rays of the elbow were negative yesterday, and the injury was diagnosed as a strain.

Brett Retains Wide Margin

June 21, 1977

George Brett, Kansas City Royals' third baseman, continued to hold a comfortable lead in the latest tabulations for the All-Star Game, which were released from the office of Bowie Kuhn, baseball commissioner, yesterday.

Brett, who started in the game for the American League last year, has accumulated 538,729 votes to far outdistance Graig Nettles, New York Yankees third baseman, who has 321,143.

The American League will play the National League July 19 at Yankee Stadium.

1977

july 13, 1977

by The Kansas City Star

Brett Won't Pass All-Star Game

George Brett, Royals third baseman and leading vote-getter at his position for the American League All-Star team, will definitely play next Tuesday in the game against the National League in Yankee Stadium unless he is injured again, a Royals spokesman said today.

There has been some question as to Brett's status because twice this season he has been sidelined because of elbow injuries, one requiring hospitalization for five days in late June.

"But he's playing every day now," said Dean Vogelaar, Royals director of public relations, "and he wants to play in the All-Star Game. Unless he suffers another injury between now and then, we're planning on his being there."

Despite his injuries, he was still one of five American League players to receive three million votes from the nation's baseball fans.

This will be Brett's second straight year as an American League starter. In his first All-Star Game last season, he went hitless but drew a base on balls in three plate appearances.

Despite his injuries, he was still one of five American League players to receive three million votes from the nation's baseball fans, who voted in record numbers this year. Brett drew 3,058,453 votes to easily outdistance Graig Nettles of the Yankees. Rod Carew of Minnesota, the first AL player to cross the four-million vote mark, catchers Carlton Fisk of Boston and Thurman Munson of the Yankees and outfielder Carl Yastrzemski of the Red Sox were the others.

1977

by The Kansas City Star

Georgie Steals a Page from the Kissing Bandit

George Brett, exposed as a bashful bachelor by baseball's kissing bandit and stripper extraordinaire, has settled the score.

Three weeks ago, the Royals' star third baseman was the target of a playful attack by Morganna Cottrell, an exotic dancer with a reputation for charging onto baseball fields and kissing players.

"Now we're even," Brett grinned last night after showing up at the Old Chelsea Theatre in the River Quay where Morganna was performing, marching onto the stage and, to the cheers of a sparse crowd, giving the stripper a kiss of his own.

The 24-year-old, gap-toothed Brett had vowed revenge since Morganna planted one of her patented puckers on him August 22 as he prepared to bat against Baltimore.

"It was just something to do in fun, that's all," said Brett, who had backed away in apprehension when Morganna approached him on the field. "She's a super lady."

Morganna is caught in the act during one of her numerous attempts to steal a kiss from George Brett.

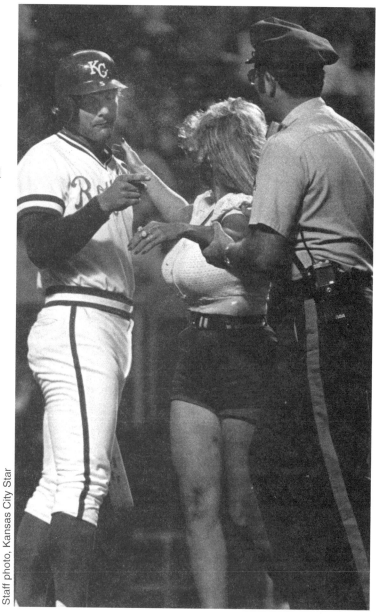

Staff photo, Kansas City Star

by Mike **DeArmond**

Game 5 Started with Bench-Clearing Brawl

Game No. 5 of the American League playoffs may have ended with a fizzle for the Royals, but it got off to a resounding bang as George Brett and Graig Nettles kicked off a bench-clearing brawl in the first inning.

Brett, tripling into center field to drive in the Royals' first run of the game, said he was kicked in the face by Nettles and came up swinging. Brett, still boiling over the incident after the game, said, "I was in the right. I asked a few reporters who had seen the instant replay, and I'm in the right.

"I'm an aggressive player. I'll do anything to win, but I don't start fights."

"What you gonna do when someone kicks you in the face? You gonna lay there and say 'kick me again?' No," Brett spat out, surrounding the denial in obscenities. "If the same thing happens next year, I'll do it again. He kicked me and I slugged him, but I didn't come into him dirty or anything—like Thurman (Munson) did to me in New York. He came in high, going after my knees."

"Nettles thought he was pushed," Yankees manager Billy Martin said. "And Brett came up swinging. Springstead (Marty, the third base umpire) told me he wasn't going to throw Brett out. This is a championship game and it's not the time to be throwing players out. If this game would have been played in July, Brett would have been gone."

"It's a basic stand-up slide. I do it a hundred times a year," Brett said. "I came up sliding hard. He hit me or something and I slugged him. I don't even know if I hit him."

Royals coaches calm Brett down after a fight with Graig Nettles in the first inning of game five.

Staff photo, Kansas City Star

Brett on All-Star Team

The Associated Press American League All-Star team bypasses the Royals as much as the one published last week by *The Sporting News.*

Hal McRae of the Royals was the choice of the players, coaches and managers for the designated hitter role on *The Sporting News* team. Yesterday the writers and broadcasters picked Jim Rice of Boston.

But the media, which participated in the AP poll, selected George Brett of the Royals at third base ahead of Graig Nettles of New York, who was the choice of those voting for *The Sporting News.*

The rest of the AP team: Catcher—Carlton Fisk, Boston; first base—Rod Carew, Minnesota; second base—Willie Randolph, New York; shortstop—Rick Burleson, Boston; outfield—Larry Hisle, Minnesota; Ken Singleton, Baltimore; and Bobby Bonds, New York.

The writers and broadcasters apparently put the emphasis on hitting with little regard to running, fielding and throwing.

Brett claimed 232 votes and Nettles 135 to leave Butch Hobson of Boston (45) and Toby Harrah of Texas (4) in the dust. Rice outdistanced McRae, 291-49, for the D.H. honor.

The Brett-Nettles situation is complex. Nettles had a better defensive season than Brett, socked more homers (37-22) and drove in more runs (107-88). But Brett, who led off most of the season, swatted away at .313, 58 percentage points better than the Yankee slugger. Even though Brett played 45 less because of injuries, he scored more runs than Nettles, 105-99.

George Brett was selected to the Associated Press AL All-Star team at third base, but another standout Royal, Hal McRae (right), was not selected.

Staff photo, Kansas City Star

1977: Boy, Did This One Hurt

It was the most bitter pill.

To this day, George Brett never hesitates. The best team he ever played on was the 1977 Royals.

They compiled a 102-60 record, the best in the major leagues. They won 16 in a row and 24 of 25 in one stretch late in the season. And, the Royals never were behind in the playoff series against the New York Yankees until the very end.

But that's when it mattered. And that's why it hurt.

In the fifth game, after the Yankees scrambled back from trailing 1-0 and 2-1 in the series, the Royals literally fought their way to a 3-1 lead heading into the eighth inning.

Brett was in the middle of the fight, too, of course. He wound up under a pile of Yankees after his aggressive slide into third base touched off combat with New York third baseman Graig Nettles in the first inning.

The Yankees scored a run in the eighth, making it 3-2, but the Royals took the field in the ninth needing only three outs for their first American League pennant. Pitching ace Dennis Leonard entered the game in relief to nail it down.

Instead, it slipped agonizingly away. A bloop single and a walk. A grounder that dribbled through the infield and another bloop hit. Finally, Brett's throwing error, and it was 5-3.

I visualized champagne and staying out until 3 in the morning two days in a row. Now I've got to make plans for the winter.

—George Brett

"The Yankees already had gone ahead by then," Brett said. "I was so mad, I didn't even know what I was doing. I almost threw the ball out of the stadium."

The dream died in the bottom of the ninth on Royals shortstop Fred Patek's wicked shot down the third-base line that Nettles turned from a double into a game-ending double play.

"I visualized champagne and staying out until three in the morning two days in a row," Brett said afterward. "Now I've got to make plans for the winter."

Fred Blocher, Kansas City Star

George Brett could roll out of bed on Christmas morning and hit a line drive.

**—John Schuerholz,
Royals general manager**

1978-79

A Team Player

The 1978 season began with a bang, literally, as George Brett's aggressive play turned sour for him. In an attempt to break up a double play at second base, Brett collided with Milwaukee Brewers shortstop Tim Nordbrook and suffered a partial separation of his left shoulder, sidelining him for more than two weeks.

Brett came back swinging and was elected to the American League All-Star team for the third time in his career. But determined as he was to lead the Royals to an American League championship, the New York Yankees defeated the Royals in the playoffs for the third straight time.

After the disappointing finish to the 1978 season, Brett had high hopes for the 1979 season. His off-season activities included, among other things, competing in the annual Superstars competition against other professional athletes and traveling with the Royals caravan around the Kansas City area to thank the fans. Brett's enthusiasm carried him into the season, and he was selected to the All-Star team for the fourth time. Nevertheless, the Royals came up short in the end, and had to settle for a second-place finish in the AL West.

april 30, 1978

by Steve Richardson

Brett Injured;
Out Two to Three Weeks

1978-79

Staff photo, Kansas City Star

George Brett, the Royals' All-Star third baseman, will be lost to the team for at least two to three weeks. That was the word late Saturday night after Brett was admitted to St. Luke's Hospital with what the Royals described as a partial separation of his left shoulder.

Brett suffered the injury in the first inning when he broke up a double play at second base.

The news brought a sudden sense of relief to the tone of conversation in the Royals' clubhouse. Earlier it was feared the injury might be worse.

Royals tend to an injured George Brett after he collided with Brewers shortstop Tim Nordbrook.

"Dr. (Paul) Meyer (the Royals team physician) just looked at the X-rays," said Manager Whitey Herzog. "He says a partial separation, two to three weeks out, which is pretty lucky. Well, he (Brett) missed 17 days after a fight last year. That's why we have Terrell (Jerry)."

"If it (Brett's injury) was a break," Herzog continued, "he would have been out seven or eight weeks. And he was coming out of the slump, oh yeah. He was hitting the ball last night. But these things just happen. He slid straight into the bag and Nordbrook (Tim, the shortstop) must have come down on his shoulder with his knee."

may 4, 1978

by Cathie Burnes

Brett Makes Plans to Return to Lineup

Leave it to George Brett, the Royals' irrepressible third baseman, to sacrifice one goal in order to make a point.

He had wanted to play all 162 games this season because he had been sidelined so often last year.

Brett thinks if his shoulder progresses the way it has the last two days he may be back at the third base position when the Yankees come calling at Royals Stadium a week from Friday.

"I think I'll be out of here tomorrow," Brett said. "I've had heat treatments and shock treatments on the shoulder."

He has made the most of his hospital stay. Friends have been bringing him his favorite foods; his favorite tobacco and a makeshift spitoon (a Missouri Tiger soft drink cup) rest at his side while he watches the Royals play. And flowers? His room at St. Luke's Hospital is beginning to resemble a floral garden.

"My mother and dad have called every day and the conversation has been the same each time. My mother keeps asking me if I need anything and I keep telling her, 'Mom, it's not realistic for you to fly 1,600 miles to bring me Red Man (his favorite chewing tobacco).'"

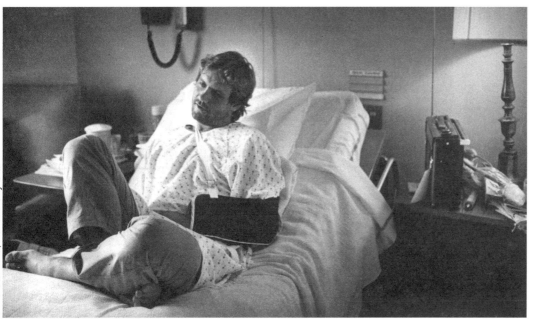

Chris Cannella, Kansas City Star

Brett talks with the press from his hospital bed about his plans to return to action after his recovery from a shoulder injury.

1978-79

by **The** Associated Press

Brett Unloads for Namesake

George Brett's devil-may-care image took a tumble Monday night when he slammed one of the longest home runs of his life and dedicated it to G.B. Peatrowsky of Fremont, Neb.

There were no home-plate ceremonies or postgame speeches. But the All-Star third baseman simply said later he hit the home run for young Peatrowsky.

Brett said he never heard of him until he arrived at the stadium Monday afternoon. It was then he found a letter and a picture of a newborn baby boy waiting for him.

"Dear Mr. Brett," said the letter, "I don't know if you'll receive this, but..."

The note from Mrs. Peatrowsky went on to say that her husband was "such a big fan of yours" that when their son was born in January he insisted they name him George Brett Peatrowsky.

"We wanted you to enjoy our happiness," the note concluded, and inside was a picture of young George Brett Peatrowsky.

"Some people might laugh at that, but I'm not," Brett said. "I take that as a compliment—a heck of a compliment. What that means is somebody thinks enough of me to want their son to be like me. That's about as high a compliment as a man can pay another man, you know? I don't take it lightly."

George Brett Peatrowsky may grow up and watch a lot of baseball games before he sees a home run as long as the one that was hit for him in the first inning Monday night. Estimated at 415 feet, it splashed into the upper tier of the water display behind the right-field fence.

It may be fitting that George Brett Peatrowsky is named after one of the most aggressive, hard-nosed players in the American League. In the snapshot, he has his eyes squeezed shut and both hands balled up into tiny fists.

"Yeah," grinned Brett, "some of the guys noticed that too."

by Sid Bordman

Sad Brett Does His Part

SAN DIEGO, Calif.—George Brett couldn't hide his disappointment after the American League again lost to the National League in the All-Star Game Tuesday night.

But the Royals' third baseman had self-satisfaction.

"That's the way we play every day," said Brett when praised for his hitting and aggressiveness in the early innings of the 7-3 loss at San Diego Stadium.

"Somebody asked me if I wasn't playing like a National Leaguer when I went for two in the first inning. I told the guy, 'No, that's the way our ballclub plays.'"

Brett, who had not hit safely in his two previous All-Star Games, changed that script in the first inning against Vida Blue when he followed a leadoff triple by Rod Carew of Minnesota with a looper to left-center. He challenged George Foster's arm—and beat the throw. Brett moved to third on a ground ball and scored on Carlton Fisk's popup to Joe Morgan, the second baseman, in shallow right field.

"I figured I'd have a shot at scoring,"

> **Somebody asked me if I wasn't playing like a National Leaguer when I went for two in the first inning. I told the guy, 'No, that's the way our ball club plays.'**
>
> **—George Brett**

Brett said, "so I went. We wanted to play aggressively."

Again in the third, Carew tripled to left-center, and Brett made it 3-0 with a sacrifice fly to Foster on the warning track in left-center.

"I thought that had a chance to hit the fence," said Brett. "I hit it pretty good. I guess I should have hit it higher and given Foster a longer look at the fence. Carew hit his higher."

Two innings later, Brett singled to right off Steve Rogers and then stole second base.

"Just cause the NL says it plays tough doesn't mean we don't," said Brett, who shared the starring role with Carew on the AL team. "I thought we'd take it to 'em. I thought we had 'em early. I never lost the feeling we'd win. We had faced Vida Blue before and knew what to expect. They had faced Rich Gossage, and knew what to expect.

"Ten years from now, this game will look like a rout. But the people here tonight and the people who watched it on television will know it wasn't."

by Mike DeArmond

Brett: We're Not Out of It Yet

NEW YORK—On a three-home run day that will burn in his memory for a lifetime, George Brett found himself talking of tomorrow . . . of false gods and prophets of doom, of what might have been but in the end wasn't—again.

In much the same fashion that they had won two previous playoff series with the Royals, the New York Yankees struck late for victory Friday afternoon. This time it was Thurman Munson's two-run home run over the distant left-field wall in the eighth inning that gave the Yankees a 6-5 triumph. New York now has to win either tonight or Sunday to clinch its third straight American League championship.

"It wasn't the fifth game," Brett said, quietly defiant. "There will be a tomorrow. When we lost the fifth games before, then there was no tomorrow. This time there is."

Ron Guidry, the ace of the New York pitching staff stands in the way of that tomorrow, of course.

"Realistically," Brett said, "Ron Guidry is not God. He is beatable. He's 25-3 and he's the best pitcher in the American League. But if we go out there and play the way we did today we've got a chance to win. And believe me, we're going to play that way."

Brett put Catfish Hunter pitches over the right-field fence in his first three times up. The first one came on the second pitch of the game, giving the Royals a 1-0 lead. Brett's second shot settled into the seats in the third, giving the Royals a 2-1 lead. And the third home run came leading off the fifth, drawing Kansas City into a 3-all tie.

Those were the opportunities the Royals took advantage of. But there were times—and many of them—that they turned a deaf ear to opportunity's knock.

In the second, Pete LaCock reached third with one down and was stranded. In the third, Kansas City loaded the bases with two down and left 'em loaded. In the sixth, LaCock tripled leading off and couldn't make it home.

Teammate Paul Splittorff, who pitched $7\ ^1/_3$ innings before giving way to Doug Bird and then Al Hrabosky, allowed as how "It's too bad we didn't win it for George. He had one hell of a game."

But Brett would have nothing of such sentiment.

"It's not what an individual does, it's whether you win or lose," said the Kansas City third baseman. "Even if I go 20-for-20 in the playoffs I don't get a check for $30,000 and everybody else get $10,000. I would rather hit one (home run) and have us win 7-1. I said, 'I hope this isn't a dream,'" Brett noted, recalling his comment after home run No. 3.

And that's the way it might have been.

"It could be a nightmare," Brett added.

And that's closer to what it was.

1978–79

january 25, 1979

by Rich Sambol

George Brett as Refreshing as Breath of Spring Air

Potholes are not my favorite subject. They wreck suspension systems, bend rims, flatten tires. You have to hold on to your steering wheel for dear life.

Hit one and you may wind up in the slush, on the side of the road, in a ditch.

Driving to work becomes work. Forty miles an hour here, 30 there, when the speed limit sign reads 55. Ah, for a nice spring day when the wind is blowing gently from the south, not roaring from the north.

Maybe, by then, Rod Carew will have been bought by the New York Yankees and maybe the Yankees will have changed their nickname to the Millionaires.

But no matter what happens, the Kansas City Royals are going to have to contend with the Yankees again and get out of their rut if they are to bring the first-ever World Series to Kansas City.

George Brett, for one, thinks it can be done.

"One of these days we are going to beat them," said the third baseman of the Royals. "And when we do, we are going to keep on beating them.

"This is the year, or maybe next year, when we set up our dynasty. Unless the Yankees add three or four 20-game winners they will be beaten out for the pennant. They might not even get there. The Red Sox may beat them."

Brett is an outspoken young man, one of the stars of the game, a superstar in fact. He is involved in the Superstars competition again this year.

He was on the nationally televised show last Sunday and qualified for the 16-man final that will be contested in early February. That final will be aired sometime in the early spring.

"I just wanted to see how good an athlete I really am," he said with a grin.

Brett is a great hitter, young, good looking and likable. He'll do anything to make the Royals a better team—hit and run, hit a homer, steal a base.

He'll even beat the boondocks to sell a ticket, like he did a couple of weeks ago on the Royals' Caravan through Kansas and Nebraska.

The caravan's function isn't to sell tickets. The idea is to bring the players to fans in outlying areas, give the people who pay a chance to meet the guys they cheer through the spring and summer.

"The Royals do this each year and it's a lot of fun," Brett said while in Manhattan, Kan. He, along with pitcher Steve Busby and utility man Jamie Quirk, were in a troupe that also attended a Kansas State basketball game that night.

When they were introduced to the crowd, they were greeted with a standing ovation. The reaction at Ahearn Field House was in keeping with what Brett anticipated an hour earlier.

"Thirty-five percent of the people who

1978–79

George Brett enjoys reaching out to his fans. "I don't know why a guy wouldn't like to do this," he says of the Royals' tradition of visiting fans around the area.

come to a game in Kansas City are not from Kansas City," Brett said. "If I were to go on one of these things and nobody showed up, I wouldn't do it. But in Topeka there were about 1,000 people left after we had been there two hours."

Brett is just folksy enough to be right at home. His smile is contagious.

"I'm not good enough to miss one of these things," he said. "I've been to all of the biggies—Hiawatha, Holton, some of the real big towns. I've been to some I've never heard of. A couple of years I got to go to Falls City."

He takes his role seriously, though.

"I don't know why a guy wouldn't like to do this," he said. "If you can't sacrifice a week for your employer, you shouldn't be playing."

He was like a breath of fresh spring air. Now, if the city would just fix the streets . . .

by Del Black

Brett One of Three Players Chosen for AL All-Star Team

Third baseman George Brett, second baseman Frank White and catcher Darrell Porter represent the all-time high for Royals elected to play in the midsummer classic, which will be staged one week from tonight in Seattle's Kingdome.

Brett, who with shortstop Fred Patek was the choice of the fans last year, will be making his fourth consecutive start.

"You've got to keep playing good every season to make it," Brett said when it was hinted that at only 26 he has dominated voting for his position. "I don't think I'd have made it if I hadn't come around after that slow start."

It's Over!
Royals Lose, 6-5

By Del Black
October 1, 1979

Royals Stadium on Sunday afternoon was not the same as it had been the previous three seasons, when Kansas City was playing its final game of the regular season while uncoiling in the wake of a championship and gearing for the American League playoffs.

Instead of a fourth consecutive West Division championship, the Royals had the runner-up spot locked up when they played Oakland, which pulled out the 6-5 victory.

For all, except the four major-league divisional winners, most of the talk in clubhouses Sunday revolved around off-season hunting, fishing and golf trips.

1978 - 79

In 1980, I missed hitting .400 by five hits and the first thing my father says is, 'You mean to tell me you couldn't get five more blankety-blank hits?' But that's the way he was, because if he knew I was ever satisfied with what I did, my performance would not have continued to be as good.
—George Brett

1980

The Quest for .400

Brett was having a solid year when he was sidelined in June by an ankle injury. Although he was voted to the All-Star team for the fifth consecutive time, his injury kept him from playing.

Brett returned to play in July and slugged his way into August. On Aug. 18, Brett brought his average to .401, sparking a quest that would transcend the game of baseball. Everywhere he went, microphones were shoved in Brett's face, and he became the focus of the entire season. The pressure was coming from all directions, from his team, the fans, even from himself. In the end, the pressure was too much. Brett ended the season at .390—still the highest average since Ted Williams' .406 in 1941.

In the meantime, the Royals were having a remarkable season. They ended their "Yankee frustrations" by sweeping the Yanks in three games of the American League Championship Series, sending them to their first World Series. They met their match in the Phillies, who ultimately defeated them in six games. Brett ended his season on a happier note, though, when he was voted the AL Most Valuable Player for 1980.

by Mike DeArmond

Brett Finds Niche as Royals Win 7-3

Hitting a baseball is a lot like sitting back in a comfortable easy chair for George Brett. If the chair is comfortable, Brett sits. If he feels comfortable at the plate, Brett hits like few others in the game of baseball.

Well, Brett was comfortable Sunday afternoon. "Probably better than I've felt since I got hurt (a bruised heel)," said Brett, who doubled twice and hit his third home run of the season in the Royals' 7-3 victory over the California Angels.

The victory was the Royals' fourth straight and gave them a sweep of the three-game series over the quickly sinking defending champions of the American League West Division.

Before the game, Brett complained he couldn't develop any consistency at the plate. "One time I feel good, the next time I don't," he said.

"When you're not comfortable, you find yourself thinking about what he's (the pitcher) trying to do to you."

"When I hit the best, I'm comfortable and I don't care what they're going to throw."

Brett's 3-for-5 game, including three runs batted in that gave him the team lead at 24, boosted his batting average 15 points to .274.

"I was back on my heels a little bit," Brett said. "Today, I made a point to stay on the balls of my feet and not crouch so much."

George kisses Muriel Kauffman, wife of Royals owner Ewing Kauffman.

Keith Myers, Kansas City Star

1980

by Rich Sambol

Brett Plans to Return to Lineup on Thursday

George Brett plans to start at third base Thursday in the Royals' first game after the All-Star break.

"I feel good," Brett said Saturday after taking 20 minutes of batting practice before the Royals played Seattle. "I've been hitting about four days, and everything seems to be on schedule."

Brett has not played since June 11, when he suffered a torn ligament in his right ankle. He was hitting .337 at the time.

The Royals' first game after the All-Star break will be against the Detroit Tigers at Royals Stadium. Until then, Brett will continue hitting and running, working on a program intended to prepare him for playing every day.

"I put on a couple of pounds," Brett said. "I was in the hospital a week and on crutches another week. I couldn't go out and do the exercises I needed to do."

Gura Named All-Star; Brett to Miss Game

July 2, 1980
By Mike McKenzie

George Brett, Royals third baseman, was supposed to be in the All-Star lineup, voted there by fans a fifth consecutive year. But he revealed Tuesday he will attend the game as a spectator while visiting family in nearby Hermosa Beach, Calif.

Brett went out of the lineup June 10 with an injury to ligaments in his right foot from a late slide into second base. He is eligible to be removed from the disabled list, and started taking full-speed batting practice Tuesday after a visit to a therapist.

1980

august 18, 1980

by Mike DeArmond

Brett Slugs Way past .400 Mark

Double Sends Statisticians Scrambling for the Books

Life slowed to the flicker of a silent movie, the ball caught as if in a strobe light, flying in fitful spurts to bounce once short of the left-field warning track, up again off the outfield wall.

A double that swept the bases clean of Royals. The hit that raised George Brett's batting average to .401.

There will be other games for those on hand at Royals Stadium for Kansas City's 8-3 victory Sunday over the Toronto Blue Jays. There will be other games for George Brett and his teammates in this American League baseball season that still has 45 games to run before the cooling winds of October supplant this muggy month of August.

But this day, this one moment in the eighth inning of an otherwise meaningless game of 1980, will be long remembered by all as nothing less than a game of games and perhaps as much as a harbinger of history.

"Goose bumps," said Brett, Royals' third baseman who has hit safely in 29 consecutive games and has crossed the .400 batting barrier no man has bettered over the course of a season since Ted Williams hit .406 for the Boston Red Sox in 1941.

Brett's movement past the .400 mark has sent statisticians all around the country scurrying to find the last hitter to breach .400 this late in the season. Since Williams, it is believed the closest was Rod Carew, who was hitting .400 July 8, 1977. Carew, then with the Minnesota Twins and now with the California Angels, dropped off to .388 that season.

The day began for Brett as any other day. Armed with the knowledge his batting average stood at .394, Brett walked down to the Royals' bullpen to hit balls off a stationary batting tee.

Through six innings, in fact, the game was like any other with the minor exception the Royals and Blue Jays were tied 2-2.

Then in the seventh, with teammates Frank White and John Wathan on base with two outs, Brett lined his third consecutive hit on this 4-for-4 day down the right-field line. The hit scored two runs, boosted the Royals into a 4-2 lead they never relinquished on the way to their fifth consecutive victory.

But, more importantly, the hit drove Brett's batting average to .399. Suddenly, the tension, the expectation, began to build.

Would Brett get another chance? Could each and every inhabitant of the park be able to say, "I was there the day George Brett hit the .400 mark?"

"I didn't think I would," Brett said. "I was sixth up, which meant we would have to have the bases loaded when I came up or we would have a couple of runs already scored."

The former was the course followed by this unbelievable script.

1980

Brett's Quest Begins to Transcend the Game

ARLINGTON, Texas—
Monday began for George Brett
the way Sunday ended . . . the way
today began . . . the way the coming days will begin and end.

A microphone was thrust in
his face. A notebook was shoved
under his nose. The eye of a
television camera focused on his
every move.

"It's becoming a joke," Brett
said. "It really is."

Suddenly, the game isn't the
thing anymore; what counts is
Brett's batting surge. The Royals'
All-Star third baseman is more than
halfway to Joe DiMaggio's 56-game
hitting streak, with a string of 30.
And his batting average is .404, a
level nobody seemingly attains in
the third week in August.

Despite the feats of others
and the team accomplishments,
the subject is Brett—before, after
and during the game.

"It's a big thing, but it's not a
big thing," said Brett. "What I mean
is . . . have I said this before? . . . I'm
not going to put pressure on
myself. How many times have I
said that?"

"About 20," he was told.

Fred Blocher, Kansas City Star

RICHARD L. BERKLEY
MAYOR

George Brett speaks to the city council after receiv-
ing a resolution from them honoring him for his
.400-plus batting average

by Mike DeArmond

As Days Dwindle, Brett Drama Builds

He pulls a batting helmet to the tops of his ears, yanks a bat from the rack and strides to the center of his world.

Arriving at the plate, he taps the dirt from his cleats and breaks the rhythmic sway of his batting stance, driving the baseball past an infielder, over an outfielder, sometimes over the fence.

The vision runs countless laps around the inside of George Brett's head.

Tuesday, though, the reality again was that of the helmet remaining on the dugout steps and the bat staying in the rack. The only striding Brett did was to traverse the short distance from the water cooler to his locker.

For most Royals, the Tuesday night rainout of the scheduled game against California was a rare second straight day off. For Brett, it was his 10th day off since tendinitis in his right wrist sidelined him September 7 in Cleveland.

Another 10 days out of the lineup is something Brett can ill-afford if he hopes to become the first man since Ted Williams in 1941 to hit .400 or better in the majors.

Brett knows he can't sit idle much longer.

"If I miss this home stand (six games against California and Oakland, winding up Sunday), it would be very, very tough," Brett said.

Keith Myers, Kansas City Star

The scoreboard at Royals Stadium served as a constant reminder of Brett's batting average throughout the 1980 season.

1980

by Mike DeArmond

Brett: The Pressure Got to Be Too Much

Becoming First .400 Hitter in 39 Years Became 'Yardstick' for Season

For more than a month he had been saying it. Over and over and over again. Each day. Every day. George Brett was not going to put any pressure on himself.

And then, on the Royals' last road trip—an 0-6 swing through the all-too-real never-never land of defeat—Brett awoke to the realization he had done that very thing.

The quest to become baseball's first .400 hitter in four decades was fading away. And Brett cared, more than he had ever wanted to admit, even to himself.

"I was a basket case on the last road trip," Brett said Tuesday night before the Royals' game against the Seattle Mariners.

Brett has always prided himself on a loosey-goosey approach to baseball. Let others approach the sport as a job; Brett saw it as a game. Zero-for-four nights at the plate rolled off his back like wind off the surf in Brett's native California.

Only suddenly, as a 3-for-20 string dropped Brett's batting average to a mere .384 after an 0-for-4 game Saturday morning in Minnesota, Brett realized he cared too much.

"I wanted it bad," Brett said. "But I wanted it too bad. I still want it bad, but I'm not going to change my life for it. This is a year I should have enjoyed more than any other in my life. But I didn't enjoy it at all."

The quest for .400 did that. It became more than a part of a wonderful season. It became the yardstick. All or nothing.

Brett now, once again, is able to take whatever comes.

"It's out of reach," Brett said of hitting .400, "but it's not over."

Closest to .400 as of 1980

1. George Brett	1980	.390
2. Rod Carew	1977	.388
3. Ted Williams	1957	.388
4. Stan Musial	1948	.376
5. Ted Williams	1948	.376
6. Rico Carty	1970	.366
7. Mickey Mantle	1957	.365
8. Stan Musial	1946	.365

1980

by Mike Fish

Royals Headed for First World Series

Brett's Homer Decisive

NEW YORK—The Royals have captured the magic of New York.

Neither a wild, screeching Yankee Stadium crowd nor ace relief pitcher Rich Gossage could save the Yankees from the Royals this time. The frustration is over.

George Brett sealed the Royals' first American League pennant with a three-run homer into the upper deck in right field. The Royals swept their old nemesis in three games of the American League Championship Series, punching their ticket to the World Series with a 4-2 come-from-behind victory Friday night.

So much for the bitter memories of '76, '77 and '78.

"I just tried to pull it and get it up in there," Brett said of his seventh-inning blast. "Defeating the New York Yankees is the biggest obstacle in our lives."

Brett's dramatic home run, a record-tying sixth in playoff competition, was the offensive blow that snapped the Yankee jinx.

"They're gonna go crazy out there (Kansas City)," said Brett. "There's real dislike between the two cities. It's a tremendous rivalry.

"It's just something they deserved. They've experienced so much frustra-

tion . . . all I know is I feel a lot happier than in '78. When I hit that I knew the game was over."

John Spink, Kansas City Star

George Brett's three-run home run sealed the Royals' first AL pennant.

1980

It's off now to either Houston or Philadelphia for the Royals.

But game three didn't come easy. The Yankees made a mad dash, loading the bases with none out in the eighth.

The Yankee Stadium crowd of 56,588 was on its feet, screaming and clapping in wild frenzy. Bob Watson started the threat with a triple that scooted past Amos Otis into the left-center gap. From there, reliever Dan Quisenberry loaded the bases with walks to Reggie Jackson and pinch-hitter Oscar Gamble.

Quisenberry, who has survived all season on the double-play ball, got behind Rick Cerone in the count 2-and-1. But the Yankee catcher lined the next delivery to shortstop U.L. Washington, who threw to second, doubling up Jackson. Pinch-hitter Jim Spencer grounded out to second, killing what would be the last Yankee threat.

"It feels good," said second baseman Frank White, the series Most Valuable Player. "Those three years we lost here we had to go back, drink our beer and sort of drink our tears. Three in a row just makes it sweeter.

"It's just an incredible feeling. You could almost hear the crowd silence when George hit that homer. You could hear their hearts die."

Quisenberry pitched the final 3 $^2/_3$ innings, earning the victory. In the end it was the slender right-hander against his well-publicized rival—Goose Gossage.

Gossage's long-awaited appearance in the series didn't come until two were out in the Royals' seventh. He came on after starter Tommy John surrendered a double to Willie Wilson and an infield hit to Washington.

Jim McTaggart, Kansas City Star

Jamie Quirk (left) and George Brett celebrate in the locker room after the Royals won the AL pennant.

It was the classic confrontation—Brett against Gossage, power v. speed.

But Brett made a shambles of the challenge when he drilled Gossage's first pitch a dozen rows deep into the right-field upper deck.

by Mike McKenzie

0-2 Royals Hanging on by Their Fingertips

PHILADELPHIA—How does Larry Gura get the first 13 batters out, and the Royals lose? How does Dan Quisenberry come in with a 4-2 lead, no men on base, and the Royals lose?

Answer: Because they both lost their "stuff" and got clubbed by the free-swinging Phillies. Because Gura "ran out of gas ... couldn't pop the fastball," according to Royals Manager Jim Frey. Because Quisenberry didn't have his usual "quick sinker" pitch, rather what he called a "poop sinker," instead of one that goes "pop."

How can George Brett play ailing, remove himself from the game, and the Royals win? How can Willie Wilson strike out the first three times at bat, five of his first eight in the World Series, and the Royals win?

Answer: They can't. Or haven't, so far.

Now the Royals feel their grip slipping.

The Phillies have had a field day with the best pitchers the Royals have to offer. Dennis Leonard and Gura, with 38 regular season victories between them, both were clobbered when apparently in control. Quisenberry had an unusually terrible outing Wednesday, suffering through a four-run eighth inning filled with line drives to the outfield walls.

Staff photo, Kansas City Star

George Brett laughs with the press after a game.

But there are more subtle factors, too.

Brett, playing with hemorrhoidal pain, said he felt if he had normal running ability, he could have stopped two hits off Gura that led to a two-run inning. " I just couldn't move, so I had to play everybody shallow at third," Brett said. "I couldn't help the club."

1980

Victory No. 2 Gives That Royal Feeling

Willie Aikens carried a big stick Saturday, and suddenly the World Series is even. Aikens, who hit two home runs in game four, now has four in the Series, and the Kansas City Royals, down two games to the Philadelphia Phillies before going home Thursday, now have two victories.

George Brett and Amos Otis added to Aikens' three RBIs, Brett driving in one run with a triple and Otis driving in another with a double, both in the first inning.

Staff photo, Kansas City Star

George Brett talks with Phillies first baseman Pete Rose. The Phillies would go on to defeat the Royals in the World Series.

Phils Savor Victory, Royals Savor Success

October 22, 1980

Both teams went into the World Series seeking their first championship. After six games, the Philadelphia Phillies were able to savor that championship, while the Royals were forced to deal with defeat.

After losing 4-1 Tuesday night in Philadelphia, several Royals said they still considered the season a success because after three failures they had beaten the New York Yankees in the American League.

1980

by Mike Fish

Brett Is AL's Most Valuable

George Brett is everything a manager would ask for in a Most Valuable Player. He just wasn't in the lineup as often as previous recipients.

Tuesday, the Baseball Writers' Association of America chose the Royals' All-Star third baseman as the American League's Most Valuable Player. In the future, however, baseball historians will recall him as the Band-Aid player, a training room miracle.

No non-pitcher has ever missed more games (45) than Brett and been acclaimed as his league's best. Not Mantle. Not DiMaggio. Not Mays.

And only the late Gabby Hartnett, who hit .344 in 116 games with the Chicago Cubs in 1935, won the award while playing in fewer games than Brett's 117.

But Brett's playing time or lack of same did nothing to cloud this, the latest and most prestigious of postseason awards.

"It's like the Cy Young if you're a pitcher. This is the one I really wanted," said Brett, who finished ahead of Reggie Jackson and Goose Gossage of the New York Yankees, second and third, respectively, in the AL voting. Royals' teammate Willie Wilson finished fourth and the Milwaukee Brewers' Cecil Cooper fifth.

Previously, Brett was named *The Sporting News* American League Player of the Year, *Baseball Magazine's* American League Performer of the Year, The Associated Press American League Player of the Year, and was recipient of Seagram's Seven Crowns of Sports Award and the Hutchinson Award.

"There's a little anxiety, you don't want to build your hopes too high," said Brett, vacationing in Palm Springs, Calif. "I remember one year (1976) I thought I had a good chance at it and didn't win. That left me a little upset. Thurman (Munson of the Yankees) got it. So I learned not to be too confident about winning."

When baseball historians look back at Brett's accomplishments, they likely will zero in on his .390 batting average—the highest since Ted Williams hit .406 in 1941—and his 118 RBIs in only 117 games. But the story may be hidden by the number of games he missed.

Brett compiled figures overall that no American League player accomplished while playing every day. And his statistics—.390, 24 home runs, 118 RBIs—are career highs.

He is the youngster who missed a fair portion of school and then jumped to the head of the class with a report card full of A's. He is the American League's valedictorian for 1980, the premier player of the game.

Without George Brett, the American League champions might have been another also-ran. The Royals' won-lost record was 23-26 in games he didn't start.

"If a guy was a 117-120 (game) type of player, then I think you could question his being MVP," said Royals Manager Jim Frey. "But George would have played every inning except for injuries.

1980

"You say 117 games, and you think of a guy who's not exactly an everyday player—a guy you're platooning. But that's not George."

"We're talking about a guy who was second in the league in RBIs (to Cecil Cooper), a guy who was still around .400 late in the season. His stats were better than guys who played 150 and 160 games."

So who or what was Brett's toughest opposition if it wasn't Jackson or Gossage? The multiple-choice answers read as such: A—bruised heel … nine games, April 29-May 6; B—torn ankle ligaments … 26 games, June 11-July 10; C—tendinitis in his right hand…nine games, Sept. 6-17; or D—hemorrhoids … three innings, game two of the World Series.

"It's funny, because when I was a kid I was always getting hurt," Brett said. "Once I started playing ball (professionally), I never had much trouble until 1977-78."

"Now it's like an every year thing. You wait for something to happen. You sit back and say, 'What's it gonna be next year?'"

"When you're out two or three times during a summer (with injuries), you learn to adjust. That last time (tendinitis), I just pretended like I was up there all the time. I played little games."

Mention Gabby Hartnett, however, and Brett draws a blank. So much for the Hall of Fame catcher.

Brett might be the best hitter baseball has to offer, a superstar talent and certainly its goodwill ambassador. But he knows nothing of Hartnett.

"I don't think I ever heard of him," Brett said. "I wasn't born when those guys were doing their thing."

1980 Final World Series Composite Box

ROYALS (23)

	AB	R	H	BI
Wilson, If	26	3	4	0
McRae, dh	24	3	9	1
G. Brett, 3b	**24**	**3**	**9**	**3**
Aikens, 1b	20	5	8	8
Porter, c	14	1	2	0
Otis, cf	23	4	11	7
Hurdle, rf	12	1	5	0
Wathan, rf-c	7	1	2	1
White, 2b	25	0	2	0
Washington, ss	22	1	6	2
Cardenal, rf	10	0	2	0
Chalk, 3b	0	1	0	0
LaCock, 1b	0	0	0	0
Concepcion, pr	0	0	0	0
Totals	**207**	**23**	**60**	**22**

PHILLIES (27)

	AB	R	H	BI
Smith, If	19	2	5	1
Rose, 1b	23	2	6	1
Schmidt, 3b	21	6	8	7
McBride, rf	23	3	7	5
Luzinski, dh	9	0	0	0
Maddox, cf	22	1	5	1
Trillo, 2b	23	4	5	2
Bowa, ss	24	3	9	2
Boone, c	17	3	7	4
Gross, If	2	0	0	0
Moreland, dh	12	1	4	1
Unser, ph-cf-lf	6	2	3	2
Totals	**201**	**27**	**59**	**26**

E: Leonard, Trillo, White 2, Christenson, Washington, Aikens 2, G. Brett, DP: Kansas City 8, Philadelphia 8, LOB: Kansas City 54, Philadelphia 41, 2B: Boone 2, G. Brett 2, Maddox 2, Otis 2, Unser 2, Schmidt, Trillo, McRae 3, Hurdle, Wilson, Smith, Bowa 3B: Aikens, Brett, HR: Otis 3 Aikens 4, McBride, Schmidt 2, G. Brett SB: Bowa 3, White, Wilson 2, Chalk, Hurdle, G. Brett. S: Washington, Gross, White, Moreland, SF: Maddox, Trillo, Wathan, Boone, Schmidt, Washington 2.

His success in the playoffs and World Series in clutch situations really elevated him from the local to the national scene. He had that national spotlight and stage to perform on. A lot of guys have been on that stage, but few have produced as he did.

—Denny Matthews,
Royals radio announcer

After battling a case of well-publicized hemorrhoids during the 1980 World Series, Brett was eager to redirect the attention away from his physical problems and toward his performance on the field.

An ankle injury interrupted Brett's season in May, and as he was waiting for an elevator in the Royals clubhouse he struck a photographer with his crutch. His temper continued to flare in June, when he took his game frustrations out on a stadium restroom during a game in Minnesota.

These were different kinds of frustrations when the players went on strike in June. Upon resuming action after the strike, Brett appeared more relaxed. Ranch life had provided him with an escape from the media and from the pressures of the game. His peaceful disposition wasn't permanent, though, and in September he had yet another confrontation with a reporter.

The split-season format worked to the Royals advantage, as they managed to wrap up a spot in the playoffs by winning the AL West for the second half of the season. Their luck ran out in the postseason when Oakland swept the Royals in the AL West Division Playoffs.

march 31, 1981

by Mike Fish

Brett's Ready to Remedy Tired Joke on His 'Disease'

FORT MYERS, Fla.—With a little more than a week before the start of the regular season, George Brett is getting ready for it, honing his skills in the batting cage and working around third base.

He is also getting ready to face a predictable stream of one-liners which will probably be directed his way—about his well-publicized bout with hemorrhoids.

Regrettably, Brett can expect to hear more than his share of hemorrhoid jokes. Every bench-jockey in the league, not to mention spirited fans in rival ballparks, will be ready for the Royals' third baseman.

"I think it might be rough at some ballparks," Brett said. "I figure if I handle it like I did in the Series, it won't be a problem. But if I start letting things people say affect me, then I think it could be a serious problem."

Of course Brett has his own plan. Just pity the first antagonist who pictures his victim as "Easy Going" George.

"I'm gonna keep some goodies in my back pocket at all times," he said. "When somebody gets on me, I'm gonna bring out a bottle of something, maybe some kind of ointment, and show it to them.

"I'll show it to them, rub my rear a lot and tell them 'I hope you get them, too.' You can hear some jerk now: 'Hey, how're your hemorrhoids?' I just hope the guy gets them so he can find out what I went through."

> **My problem's behind me now.**
> **—George Brett,**
> **after hemorrhoid surgery**

Already this spring, Brett has heard from several major leaguers who have had the same problem.

"It's really funny," Brett said. "It seems like whenever we play a new team down here, somebody tells me about his hemorrhoids. Like Lamar Johnson told me. 'I know what you went through. I had them two years ago.' Guys are coming out of the shelves now."

1981

Photographer Hit by Brett's Crutch

Kansas City third baseman George Brett struck a news photographer in the head with a crutch as Brett was leaving Royals Stadium during Thursday night's game with the Texas Rangers.

Tom Gralish, a photographer for United Press International, was struck above the right eye but was not hurt seriously. Brett was leaving for St. Luke's Hospital with an ankle injury.

Brett, who had been hurt sliding into home plate in the fourth inning, was with teammate Clint Hurdle. They were waiting for the clubhouse elevator.

"Brett stuck out his crutch and hit me with a swipe up and caught my camera on the way down," Gralish said.

"He said, 'Don't you have anything . . . better to take pictures of?' I was stunned."

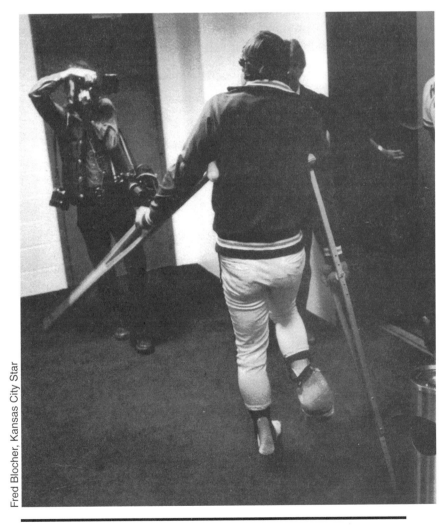

Fred Blocher, Kansas City Star

George Brett swings his crutch at a photographer while waiting for an elevator outside the Royals' clubhouse.

1981

by Mike Fish

Twins Haven't Overlooked Brett's Restroom Rampage

The Royals can expect a bill in the near future for the damage that George Brett caused in a Metropolitan Stadium restroom during Friday night's game with the Minnesota Twins.

The only question is who will reimburse the Twins: the All-Star third baseman or the Royals? After grounding out with runners on base, Brett went into a restroom behind the dugout and used his bat to break two toilets and a sink. A Twins' spokesman said the fixtures would have to be replaced, although the club will be moving next season to the Metrodome, which is under construction in downtown Minneapolis.

The restroom damage came about two weeks after Brett had struck a United Press International photographer, Tom Gralish, with a crutch. Brett swung the crutch at the photographer May 14, when Brett had injured his right ankle in a game with the Texas Rangers and was leaving Royals Stadium for X-rays at a hospital.

Joe Burke, the Royals' executive vice president and general manager, said: "We'll have to wait and see all the details before determining who's responsible for the expense. This has happened before, and it's not that uncommon. Guys have hit a wall or a trash can with their bats. It's happened in almost every stadium I've been in."

Before Monday night's game with the Seattle Mariners, Brett was visibly outraged that the restroom damage had been reported in *The Kansas City Times*. He implied that he had a right to privacy, just as an individual who might punch a hole in the wall of his home would not see his name in the newspaper.

"I don't think it's anybody's business," Brett said. "It's already written, so why should I discuss it?"

1981

june 13, 1981

by Rich Sambol

Royals Hold Out Little Hope of Quick Strike Settlement

A smiling face whizzed by Renie Martin as he waited for his luggage Friday at Kansas City International Airport.

"Way to pitch Thursday night," she said. "It was a nice way to end the season."

The Royals relief pitcher said thanks.

"A lot of people are saying things like that," Martin said. "There was a newspaper passed around on the plane, and somebody wrote 'FINAL' on the top of the American League standings."

Martin's season really could be over. He and 649 other players went on strike against major-league baseball Friday on the advice of Marvin Miller, executive director of the Major League Players Association.

"If the season is over, it's going to be an empty summer," Martin said.

"When you've been playing baseball for 15 or 16 years, it's going to be difficult to adjust.

"I don't know what to expect now. I really didn't think there would be a strike. I thought they would work something out. Apparently they didn't."

Royals Stadium will generally be off limits to the players until the strike is settled.

The players are expected to stay in Kansas City at least for the next three days. If they leave town, they will be expected to keep in touch with relief pitcher Dan Quisenberry, the Royals' player representative.

> **If the season is over, it's going to be an empty summer.**
> **—Royals reliever Renie Martin**

1981

august 17, 1981

by Mike Fish

Royals Are Back in a Pennant Race

1981

CLEVELAND—Trumpets didn't announce the Royals' return to life. There was no jumping up and down in the clubhouse, no good-natured back slapping.

After stumbling for much of the summer, the Royals—thanks to a helping hand from the split-season format—find themselves in a pennant chase.

For the first time this season, the defending American League champions moved over the .500 mark by defeating the Cleveland Indians 6-2 in the first game of the doubleheader on Sunday.

The Royals then retreated to .500 with a 4-4 record when Cleveland won the second game 8-6.

"Things look a lot different than they did in May," said Royals second baseman Frank White. "I wouldn't have believed it if somebody told me we'd play as well as we did the first night in Baltimore, especially considering the (exhibition) game with St. Louis.

"We were down from the start of the season. When you lose as much as we did, it can get contagious. Now the attitude seemed a lot different, I'm just happy to see guys running the bases more aggressively."

George Brett returned to the lineup for the first time since he injured his right thumb Thursday night against Baltimore.

Keith Myers, Kansas City Star

The hitting of George Brett helped put the Royals back in the pennant race.

august 23, 1981

by Mike McKenzie

Sitting Tall in the Saddle Proves Big Boost for Brett

Ranch Life Affords Chance to 'Lose Himself'

NEW YORK—A common sight these days in the Royals' clubhouse before or after a game: George Brett, wearing a towel, or undershorts, and honest-to-snakeskin cowboy boots.

An American League umpire, Durwood Merrill, turned Brett on to cobra hide for footwear. But it's not a charade.

Brett fancies himself an honest-to-yip-pykiyiyo cowboy.

He owns a horse, a Morgan filly named Funquest Siri, and soon he'll own a ranch near Kansas City (he won't say where). Morever, Brett has the chafed fanny and blistered memories of riding a real roundup to back his claim.

It's not unreasonable to credit some of Brett's cowboyitis for his more relaxed personality since the baseball strike ended.

During the strike, once he decided the '81 season was doomed, Brett headed for open country. For the last three years, he has spent considerable time in the off-season at a ranch near Panhandle, Texas—alias, Middle of Nowhere—owned by Mike Battle.

Battle, a boyhood friend of Ken Brett's when he attended rival California high schools, played football for the New York Jets in 1969 and 1970. He brandished a mean punt return before retiring.

"He used to run with my brothers," Brett said. "He used to bring me $80 athletic shoes from USC (Southern California).

"I just lost touch with Mike," Brett said. "I found him three years ago, way out on his ranch. He invited me out. After the World Series last year, I went with Jamie (Quirk) and Ken.

"When I'm out there, I don't have a care in the world. I'm so relaxed. I don't even know what day it is. Well, I don't even know that today ... but the point is, I can lose myself on that ranch."

Lose himself.

That has become a big thing to Brett in the last year. About a year ago, he was raising his hand above his head at second base, grinning over a double that pushed his batting average past .400: a picture frozen in many minds as symbolic of the Royals' American League championship season.

Since then, Brett has led a parade of media bounty hunters that would make any pied piper drool with envy. It has taken him to the borders of irascibility; he is angry that he can't even get angry in private anymore.

Impulsively, he lashes out with crutches at a photographer. Headlines. Impulsively, he lashes out with a bat at a toilet hidden behind a dugout ... but not hidden from headlines.

Gradually, Brett began to stay out of sight more in the clubhouse, stay on the field more during pregame practice, stay as accessible as possible without giving away all his spare moments to interviews, banquets or other personal services.

At one stage of last winter, Brett appeared in 12 cities in an 18-day span. He lit the spotlight and burned himself out on it.

In Panhandle, in Battle's chores, he had found refuge from the glare of '80. He would find it again in mid-summer when his encore had soured from a strike and a slump.

Panhandle is about 30 miles from Amarillo. "Lots of horses, cattle, wheat and flat green grass for as far as you can see," Brett described his Camelotian retreat. "You don't see much cement, and there's a whole lot of good country living."

To Brett, the best part of being there is, he is not George Brett. He is one of a large lot of Cowboy Joes.

"The guys we ride and rope with know us, and ask a few questions about baseball," Brett said. "But not anybody else. To them I'm just one of the cowboys."

Not as in Urban, either. Brett emphasized. "I've woke up in the morning and put a chew or a dip in my mouth—that's a real cowboy," he said.

"I've gone to the bathroom behind the barn where there is no toilet paper, that's a real cowboy. I've ridden, roped, branded, given shots, everything but castrated, and I would have done that but it wasn't the right time of year."

Brett laughed at the telling of how he nearly roped himself and his horse while trying to lasso a runaway calf. "That's not easy," he said.

Another moment stands out in Brett's mind.

He rode a horse, named Red Man. "I call him Ol' Red," Brett said. "We'd been riding as fast as he would go. We both got tired, and Ol' Red started ambling along—you know, shoulders rolling from side to side.

"I leaned forward and crossed my hands on the saddle, without reins. For a time there, I felt like one of those old paintings of a cowboy resting and looking out at the beautiful country, green in every direction."

"I said to myself, What the hell am I doing playing baseball? I could do this everyday the rest of my life."

Quirk, perhaps Brett's best friend and confidant, says not quite yet. But someday.

Fred Blocher, Kansas City Star

George Brett gestures to his horse, Funquest Siri, at the American Royal Horse Show.

"The ranch is a perfect place for retirement," Quirk said, "Especially for a guy like George, so famous and bothered. You have neighbors out there, but you really don't see them."

by Mike McKenzie

Brett and *Times* Reporter Scuffle at California Hotel

ANAHEIM, Calif.—Mike Fish, who covers the Royals for *The Kansas City Times*, and Royals third baseman George Brett had to be restrained from fighting each other after Monday night's 4-3 Royals victory over the California Angels.

According to several witnesses, no punches landed. Fish was scratched beneath both eyes when he was pinned against a wall by Dean Vogelaar, the Royals public relations director. Brett was pulled aside by teammates Greg Keatley and Willie Wilson.

The incident occurred about 1:30 a.m. Tuesday in a lobby hallway at the Anaheim Hyatt. Police were summoned, but no arrests were made.

Tempers flared after Brett and Vogelaar made remarks about news stories that Fish had written June 1 and 2. He had reported that Brett had broken up two toilets and a sink in a ballpark restroom in Bloomington, Minnesota.

Brett had been standing in the hotel hallway with two women friends. Fish walked by with sportswriter Alan Eskew of *The Topeka Capital Journal*, Janis Carr, a reporter formerly with *The Los Angeles Times* who will begin working September 28 for *The Kansas City Star* and Ms. Carr's sister. Brett said something to Fish related to the Minnesota story. Both agreed that the remark had been made in a joking fashion.

Then Vogelaar joined the group and Ms. Carr entered the conversation.

"I told him, 'Don't you think you put yourself into the limelight as an athlete?' And he pointed his finger in my face," Ms. Carr said. "I don't have to stand for that. I pushed his hand away. Then he pushed my face with his fingertips with some force."

Fish responded. "I said something like, 'You can't do that,' and he swung at me," Fish said.

Brett's version was similar.

"Suddenly, this girl I don't know, and who doesn't know me, starts laying into me about how I should act, and what kind of person I am," Brett said. "The more lip I got, the more excited I got.

"I told the girl, 'That's it. I've had enough,' and I pushed her a little and turned away. Some shouting occurred, things were said, minor actions were taken, then Dean did his job—peacemaker, separating us."

october 1, 1981

by Mike Fish

Royals Wrap Up Spot in Playoffs

BLOOMINGTON, Minn.— It was the kind of game that deserves a full house: the Royals and Twins, playing the last baseball contest at Metropolitan Stadium with Kansas City needing a victory to ensure a playoff position.

But only 15,900 fans chose to pay for the privilege of witnessing the end of an era that began when the Washington Senators moved to Minnesota for the 1961 season.

On a cool and dreary afternoon, Larry Gura pitched the Royals into the playoffs with a 5-2 victory. It was the Royals' fourth straight victory, and by sweeping the three-game series in Minnesota they dashed the Twins' playoff hopes.

The Royals pounded out 16 hits against the Twins. They went through four Minnesota pitchers.

A few months ago, the Royals were miles away from a pennant race. But the

Greg B. Smith, Kansas City Star

George Brett's problems with the media this season did not affect his ability to lead the Royals into the postseason.

splitting of the season gave them life.

The Royals probably will have the worst record of any club to participate in postseason play. They have an overall record of 48-51. With five games remaining, they can finish no better than two games above .500.

The low percentage distinction is now held by the 1973 New York Mets, who captured the National League East crown with an 82-79 record. They defeated the Cincinnati Reds in the league championship series, only to lose to Oakland in the seventh game of the World Series.

But for now, the Royals are alive and well. Their most pressing concern is to gain a home-field advantage by finishing ahead of the A's. If the Royals finish first in the American League West at the end of the second half of the season, the first two games of the best-of-five divisional championship series will be played at Royals Stadium.

1981

by Joe Mc Guff

Royals Take Loss Quietly; Brett Calls It Frustrating

OAKLAND, Calif.—The Royals' 1981 season ended Friday night with an unsightly 4-1 loss to Oakland. But, whatever the anguish the Royals felt, they kept to themselves.

The scene in their dressing room was somber, but otherwise there was no display of emotion.

Team owner Ewing Kauffman made a brief appearance, moving among his players and offering a few words of consolation. The Royals answered reporters' questions matter-of-factly. They said they were puzzled by their failure to hit. They said they were frustrated and disappointed and, to a degree, embarrassed.

"It's very frustrating," George Brett said. "This kind of exemplifies the way we played all year. We've played three or four good games and three or four bad ones.

"I'm embarrassed not because we lost to the A's, but because we didn't play as well as we possibly could. They beat us five times and made us go to Cleveland (for a makeup game after the regular season was scheduled to be over).

"It's embarrassing when you go out and play the way we did the last three days. It's very frustrating. We just didn't play good. I didn't swing close to my potential. Otie (Amos Otis) didn't get a hit. We couldn't put anything together."

Willie Wilson said that losing bothered him more than the errors and mistakes the Royals made.

"We got into a rut the first half (of the season). We tried so hard to come back, but we struggled all year. Nothing worked. Maybe we were just trying too hard. It was a messed up year. I'm sorry to lose, but I'm glad we'll be able to start all over again next year."

Pitcher Ken Brett Released by Royals

November 26, 1981

Veteran relief pitcher Ken Brett was given his unconditional release Wednesday by the Royals.

Brett, 33, asked for his release.

"I wasn't able to assure him of what would be available next year," said John Schuerholz, Royals' executive vice president and general manager. "We talked very briefly in my office. After my assessment, he said he'd like to have his release."

Brett appeared in 22 games last season. He had a 1-1 record and a 4.18 earned-run average.

If a tie is like
kissing your
sister, losing is
like kissing your
grandmother, with
her teeth out.

—George Brett

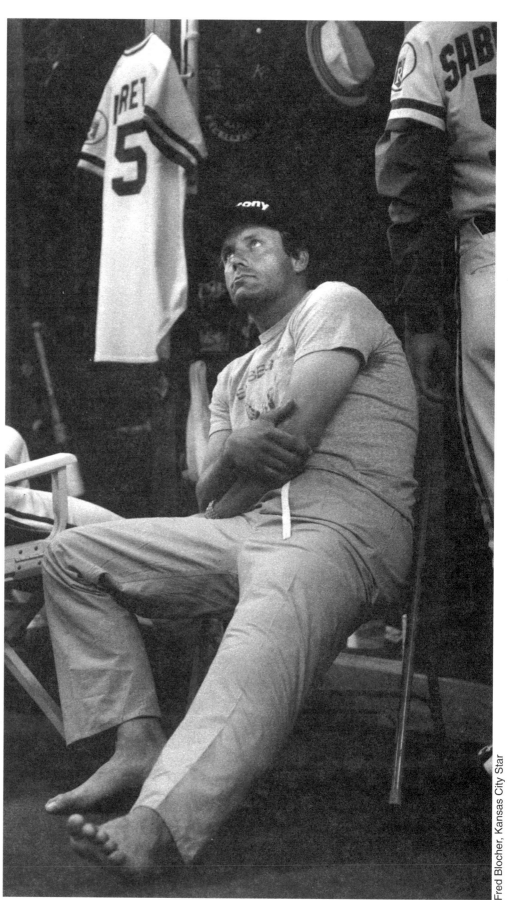

Coming Up Short

June is a month that, in the Royals' short history, had been a boomer. June of 1982 was no exception. But even though the Royal bats were on fire, June was not a good month for George Brett, but he didn't mind. "The wonderful thing about not being the star every night is being able to go my own way," he said.

On those few moments when Brett was able to go his own way, rock concerts and roping cattle were his choice leisure activities. Brett was also never completely satisfied with his position at third base day after day, and he often wanted to try a different position to "add a little excitement" to things.

But Brett created his own excitement at third base, and, after a short time off from a wrist injury, he powered his way through the rest of the season. Brett's surge was not enough in the end, and for only the second time since 1975, the Royals ended their season short of the playoffs.

june 10, 1982

by Mike McKenzie

While Royals Lead the Pack, Brett Doesn't

1982

MINNEAPOLIS—The Royals are moving out smartly. And where is George?

Royal bats are busting out all over. Kansas City has a .297 team batting average, an eight-game winning streak and a one-game lead in the American League West after beating Minnesota 8-5 Wednesday night. And where is George?

Recent history shows that when the Royals possess championship mettle, they begin to flow steadily in June and take charge of the West Division race. The same history shows that the June-to-October streaks have occurred with third baseman George Brett as leader of the pack, give or take a hot-hitting teammate or two.

Well, the Royals have begun their characteristic June boon, scoring runs in gushes. And where is George? He's hitting .290—tied for sixth among the nine regular batters on the club.

Brett isn't having a bad year, mind you. More players than not would trade for a .290 average. It's been a productive .290, too—56 hits, 12 doubles, four triples, six home runs, 27 runs batted in and five game-winning hits (including one Wednesday night). In fact, for Brett those are high numbers for this time of the year, based on most of his past.

If anything, the Royals themselves seem intent on not Letting George Do It.

On June 1, 1977, Brett was hitting .304 with one home run and 13 RBIs. The Royals were 21-23, in sixth place, 6 $\frac{1}{2}$ games out of

first. Brett finished with a .312 average, 22 home runs and 88 RBIs. The Royals went 81-37, finishing first by eight games.

On June 1, 1980, Brett showed a .301 average, three home runs and 27 RBIs. The Royals had just opened a two-game lead with a 27-18 record. Brett ended the year at .390, 24 home runs and 118 RBIs. The Royals ended up with 97 victories and a 14-game margin as champions.

Other title years—1976, 1978 and 1981's second season—reflect similar trends of the team and Brett, though not as quick paced.

Amos Otis' observation holds water, too. Statistics find teammates Otis and Hal McRae and former teammates Al Cowens and John Mayberry ahead of Brett in hitting production several times from 1976 to the present.

In '77, Cowens matched Brett's .312 average and bested him in home runs, 23, and RBIs, 112. McRae had 92 RBIs that season, four more that Brett.

Otis observed, "No doubt it takes a lot of pressure off each individual when the team isn't counting on just one person most of the time."

McRae never saw the situation as unhealthy, but he sees the present one as healthier. "Obviously the more people playing well, the better off you are," he said.

"But it helps individuals psychologically to get a little of the publicity when he's doing well, when that's spread out, there's more unity. Everybody has to get satisfaction out of going out there every day. Doing well is satisfaction; getting recognition for it is more satisfaction."

What does Brett make of the situation? Does he miss the limelight he commanded in 1980, overflowing into '81?

"No way," he said.

"I'm very honest about that, too. A lot of people might want to be the talk of the town, and hey, I want to hit .900. But, I'm so much more at ease on the field and off it now that nobody pays any attention to me."

Well, almost nobody. He, like any player, gets in on the common barrage of post-game question analyzing any given game. But, the magazine reporters from coast to coast are not flocking to his side.

Brett is no wallflower. He still cannot walk in public without attracting attention, some of which nettles him.

A lot of people might want to be talk of the town, and hey, I want to hit .900. But, I'm so much more at ease on the field and off it now that nobody pays any attention to me.

—George Brett

Before a game against the Twins this week he was asked by a Twins official to spend some pregame time with a family Brett had never met before and probably never will again.

"Am I a jerk if I refuse them?" he asked rhetorically.

Brett, while not sensational at bat, does not feel lost in the crowd with the Royals. "I'm not satisfied with my numbers, yet they are higher than usual for me this time of year. (His average, as of June 1, was .279, the lowest of the last seven years at a comparable time. Until last year's .286, he had been between .300 and .351 by June 1 since 1976.)

"And, if I look hard enough, I can see how I've been contributing several ways, such as moving runners to third several times. I'd rather bat them in, but I'm not down in the dumps over the way things are going. If we were losing, I'd probably feel different."

His all-out playing style continues. The only five games he missed this year resulted from an injury on an attempted breakup of a double play at second base. Brett's defense at third has been unusually effective, as well.

Outwardly, he seems more at ease and upbeat this season than any time since the middle of 1980 when he was aglow over the pursuit of a .400 average, a pursuit which eventually soured him considerably.

"I've only snapped once this season," he said. "That was a little snap where I just used my bat on the same trash can everybody else beats on. No toilets."

Last year Brett made headlines when he destroyed toilet property in Minnesota.

Also it was here with about a week to go in the '80 season that Brett went into a shell, refusing his daily audience with the assorted media, and "snapping" after a zero-for-four performance that sent him plunging on a night he wasn't supposed to play.

"A coach told me I'd get a rest on a Saturday morning after a night game," Brett recalled. "I didn't eat breakfast, went to the park early and horsed around, planning to spend the day in the bullpen. I saw my name in the lineup and said, 'What!' I'm not one to say I'm not ready to play, so I went out and got nothing for four against Jerry Koosman. I still had a chance (for .400) at the time, it really burned me."

From that point on through a World Series in which his hemorrhoids got more play than his hitting, and on into 1981, weighted under by disappointing hitting (.314, nonetheless), bad behavior and the strike, Brett's usual outgoing demeanor receded.

"The wonderful thing about not being the star every night is being able to go my own way," he said.

by Mike McKenzie

It'll Never Happen, but if Brett Had His Druthers . . .

He'd Travel with Blondie, Rope Some Cattle and Play Several Positions

BALTIMORE—Some days George Brett would like to be a first baseman or left fielder.

To get a good reading on that, though, you must realize that some days Brett would like to be a cowboy on the lone prairie, and some days he'd like to be Blondie's road manager and Deborah Harry's personal valet.

Brett would make a good amoeba. He then could be all kinds of Bretts in all kinds of places. Third baseman George wants to be left fielder George? Fine. Multiply. Divide. Presto!—third base AND left field. Repeat process. Eureka!—third base AND left field AND first base AND one to spare, ready for the next whim or fancy.

Will the use of Brett this season in left field and his good, sometimes outstanding, performance there now put to rest the four-year-old speculations that he fits into the Royals' future at first base?

Does he instead fit into the Royals' future at left field?

Where does he want to fit?

For the answers, let's join Brett at his dressing stall in the Royals' clubhouse. Let's not look directly at him for too long, because he is wearing antennae. You know. The kind bees have, only these antennae have little silver hearts on the tips. "A gift," he explains.

Let's also take note that Brett is a little edgy about something. Above his stall he is tacking a poster of a shock of blond hair that looks electrified and in the middle of it is singer Deborah Harry's face. Brett explains how much he enjoys her group's sound, and how irritated he was that the game the night before had kept him from being with Blondie at its concert in Kansas City.

"A quick game, and I'm backstage with them," he says. "But, no, we have to go extra innings . . ."

Brett has played eight games in left field this season. Probably he will play a few more. Late Wednesday night he seemed to be a shoo-in to play some against the Orioles this weekend, because left fielder Willie Wilson was lying on a stretcher, having taken a pitch in the cheek.

But Wilson rejoined the club Thursday in Baltimore and said some soreness was the only aftereffect he felt from the beaning by Dan Petry. On Friday he was back in the lineup card.

In the past, Brett has been frank in saying he doesn't care for his main position.

"Some days I like it, some days I don't," he said in his latest assessment. "Playing another position adds excitement for me. It breaks up the monotony of day in, day out,

1982

nine years in the same position, same stadium.

He described his feelings about left field: "Different fun, challenging, exciting, ravishing." Ravishing?

Well, anyway .... his ups and downs with third base have never reached a point of becoming a major issue. Brett never has insisted on being moved, nor has the club ever planned to move him.

Mainly he has become aggravated with third base when he wasn't playing it well. "If I had continued to make 30 errors a year like when I first came up," he said, "then I'm sure I would have said, 'Hey, look, you keep telling me I'm a good third baseman, but, I'm not comfortable here and I'd be better for the club at a different position.'

"But I think I've improved my defense enough that I could play third base for a lot of clubs, regardless of what I hit."

Talk of moving him to first base first arose in 1978 after John Mayberry departed for Toronto. Manager Whitey Herzog used Brett at first base on occasion.

"About the same as Dick has used me in left field," Brett recalled.

John Schuerholz, the club's general manager, who in those days was in charge of developing players in the minor-league system, said the Royals never had a "master plan" that moved Brett off third.

"Most of the talk about him moving to first came from him," Schuerholz said. "He started saying the same things about left field when we were in Japan, and that he'd like to wind up playing there someday."

Howser first experimented with Brett in left field when the Royals toured Japan last November. Brett had not played outfield since he was a kid, and then only once.

Dan White, Kansas City Star

Brett is attended by an ad agency assistant at a photo shoot for Trans World Airlines, Inc.

"It was an all-star game and I was a catcher," Brett said. "The other catcher was a year older than me, though, so they stuck me in right field."

Howser filed the fact that Brett played left field better than average against Japanese competition. Early this season, when injuries to Wilson and Amos Otis dictated, Brett was inserted in left field.

He has played it smoothly, making a few outstanding catches and one throw that particularly raised eyebrows. On the last trip to Cleveland, Brett threw out Toby Harrah trying to score, protecting a tie in an eventual Royals' victory.

"I was the most surprised guy in the ballpark," Brett said. "I couldn't stop laughing I was so tickled. I'm supposed to make good plays at third, and Willie and Otis are supposed to make those plays from the outfield. I played good in Japan, but this was the first time ever I came in and made a play like that. Gee whiz!"

by Mike Fish

Royals Wallop White Sox, Keep Pace with California

Brett's 3-Run Single Enough to Keep KC, Angels Tied

CHICAGO—George Brett, a missing link in the Royals' pennant chase, swooped down on the Chicago White Sox Friday night and stung them where it hurts most.

Brett, three for five, swept the bases clear with a single in a four-run fourth inning and led the Royals to a 7-1 victory.

The inning didn't lack dramatics: Brett against Jerry Koosman, bases full, runners moving and a 3-2 count. With the swing of a bat, Brett broke open a 2-1 game and kept the Royals even with the California Angels, who beat the Boston Red Sox 7-6 Friday night in the AL West Division. Both clubs are 74-54.

Brett, starting his third game after being out of action for 12 games because of tendinitis caused by bone chips in his right wrist, contributed the hit that starting pitcher Paul Splittorff needed to get past the White Sox. Brett, the Royals' third baseman, has swung the bat better than ever since his return. In three games, he is five for 12, including three doubles.

"It felt real good having people shake my hand," said Brett, the center of attention in the visitors' clubhouse.

Royals (left to right) Jamie Quirk, George Brett and Willie Aikens take time for a little joking around at a workout at Royals Stadium.

1982

by Jonathan Rand

Climb Back Too Steep for Royals in AL West

For only the second time since 1975, the Royals ended their season playing a game that meant nothing.

A 6-3 loss to the Oakland A's on Sunday at Royals Stadium left the Royals with a 90-72 record, an impressive turnaround from a 50-53 finish last year but three victories short of a division title.

It was convenient to blame the Royals' blues last season on the player's strike, former Manager Jim Frey or post-World Series complacency.

The Royals, in truth, were a mediocre team in 1981 and needed a lot of off-season renovation. Despite a fatal September slide of 10 losses in 11 games, they finished 1982 with the fifth-best record in major-league baseball.

"It wasn't quite good enough," Manager Dick Howser said. "More positive things came out of it than negative things, but it doesn't mean a whole lot if you don't win it."

The Royals jumped into contention because several bats that slept through 1981 jumped to life; the bullpen became more than a one-man show with Mike Armstrong, Bob Tufts and Bill Castro joining relief ace Dan Quisenberry; John Wathan became a respectable catcher and right fielder Jerry Martin was acquired in a trade, improving the defense; and Howser made better use of his personnel than Frey, reverting to the Royals' traditional style of manufacturing runs out of line drives and aggressive base running.

Vintage hitting years were enjoyed by designated hitter Hal McRae, second baseman Frank White, shortstop U.L. Washington and left fielder Willie Wilson. Center fielder Amos Otis had his best year since 1979.

A team enjoying peak seasons from so many players ought to win a pennant, as the Royals did in 1980 when they had a bumper crop of prime batting averages.

So why did the Royals fall short? Injuries, obviously, were a drawback, allowing Howser his regular lineup in only 43 of the 162 games, taking away 34 starts from his pitchers and putting 12 players on the disabled list.

But injuries, primarily, did not undo the Royals. Mediocre starting pitching was the main villain, with a lack of bench power an accomplice. John Schuerholz, Royals executive vice president and general manager, spent the off-season improving both areas . . . but not enough to beat the California Angels in the American League West Division.

1982

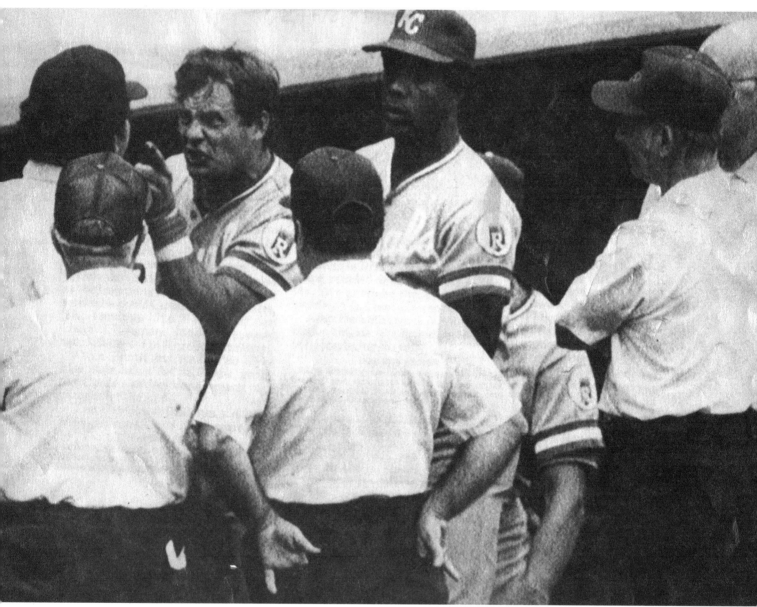

The next thing you know, they drop the bat down and measure it on home plate. As soon as they did that I said, 'You know, if they call me out, I'll kill them. I'll run out on the field and I'll kill them all right now.'

—George Brett on the "pine tar" incident

A Sticky Situation

After surviving a batting slump in which he had two hits in 32 at-bats, Brett went on a tear through the season. Interrupted only by a hamstring injury in June, Brett put up numbers rivaling his illustrious 1980 numbers. By July, he was hitting .364 with 17 home runs and 57 RBIs.

The focus was taken off Brett's achievements and placed on his temper weeks later when he hit a home run that put the Royals up 5-4 over the Yankees. Moments after he crossed home plate, umpire Tim McClelland examined Brett's bat and called him out because of excessive pine tar on the bat's handle. The famed events that followed in which Brett lost control have come to be known to baseball fans as simply the "pine tar" incident.

Brett's home run later was reinstated and the game was resumed a month later, with the Royals coming out on top. By September, however, the Royals were out of playoff contention and playing only for pride.

by Mike Fish

Brett, McRae Can Laugh Now after Breaking Spring Slumps

BALTIMORE—It was time to laugh and down a couple of beers. Cameramen and media types surrounded George Brett and Hal McRae after the Royals' 7-2 victory over the Baltimore Orioles in their season opener Monday afternoon. The two were having a good time, cracking one-liners about their surprising success.

There were several hitting stars— Willie Wilson and Willie Aikens among them— but the most unlikely characters turned out to be Brett and McRae. Neither hit a lick the last 10 days of spring training. Third baseman Brett, who has a .316 lifetime average, headed north with two hits in his last 32 at-bats. Designated hitter McRae, who lives by his bat as evidenced by his league-leading 133 RBIs in 1982, left Florida with .176 average.

"They both have a lot of pride," Royals Manager Dick Howser said. "When they didn't hit or drive in runs maybe they were embarrassed. A guy like Mac doesn't hit .170 something and come into a game confident."

But when the regular season started Monday afternoon, Brett and McRae rediscovered their wonderful hitting strokes. The magic was back.

"You saw that act down there (in training camp in Fort Myers, Fla.)" said Brett, who also made two fine fielding plays at third base. "I think in the beginning I was real excited about being there and hit the ball good. Then it got monotonous. Maybe after the first 10 (exhibition) games my concentration wasn't that good.

"Hey, I was starting to get a little worried. Rocky Colavito and I have been talking about it. Basically, I think I was just lazy. This was different—50,000 people and playing for something other than just to get out of Florida.

"I mean, I woke up at 4 this morning excited about going to the ballpark. I never woke up in Fort Myers at 4 looking to go to Terry Park."

It may be too early to tell whether Brett is out of the hitting blues, but he must have convinced Orioles starter Dennis Martinez. Brett doubled in the first inning off Martinez, later scoring the game's first run, and hit a towering two-run home run in the third inning into the right-field seats. And as a sign that Brett had the Orioles' respect, he received an intentional walk with two outs in the eighth and the Royals leading 7-2.

1983

may 7, 1983

by Mike Fish

Brett Returns, Extends Hitting Streak to 17

TORONTO—It is not "man-bites-dog" news when a baseball player is scratched from the lineup for a week because of a pulled hamstring muscle. Nothing big, right? But there's a catch when the player is All-Star third baseman George Brett, who happened to be enjoying the finest start of his career.

Brett reappeared in the Royals' lineup for the series opener Friday night against the Blue Jays. Brett strained a hamstring muscle in his left leg last Friday night running the bases against the Cleveland Indians, causing him to sit out the next five games. The Royals were 2-3 during his absence.

"It's been somewhat frustrating because this is the first time in a long start," Brett said. "There are times when you're swinging the bat so bad you're hoping for an injury to get your mind off the game. This has been quite the opposite."

Indeed, his numbers this spring have been remarkable. Brett extended his hitting streak Friday night to 17 games and has a .456 batting average, second best in the American League. Two weeks ago in a series against the Blue Jays at Royals Stadium, Brett had five hits—including three doubles and a triple—in 11 at-bats.

At the time of his injury, Brett led the major leagues in average (.460), slugging percentage (.921), doubles (12) and runs batted in (20). He was in a near-perfect groove, seeing the ball well and driving it with authority.

Brett expects to remain in the groove, he said, because he's been able to take daily batting practice. The only thing he hasn't been able to do is run at full speed.

"I would be surprised if I didn't come back and hit well," he said. "A lot of times when you're injured you can't take batting practice. I've continued to swing the bat good in batting practice.

"I'd expect to go out and do the same kind of things. I don't see why I should have regressed at all. I just wish this thing didn't drag on for a week."

Normally, you can sit comfortably with a .460 average and expect to remain the league leader. Not this time. While Brett nursed himself well, Rod Carew of the California Angels raised his average to .500 after Friday's games.

"I picked up the paper today and saw he (Carew) was hitting .480 or whatever," Brett said. "I know what he's doing, but I don't think about beating anybody for any titles. A lot of things can happen between now and the end of the season.

"He's off to a great start, I was off to a good start and a lot of other people are off to good starts. Now it's a matter of maintaining that."

1983

Brett Keeps Increasing His Power at Plate

CLEVELAND—There is the temptation to compare everything George Brett does on the field with his exploits of 1980. Even he catches himself doing it. That's one of the reasons why, he says, the last two summers weren't much fun.

This year, though, Brett is enjoying a season that in some ways could be as good as or better than his dream season. There probably won't be a chase of .400, although his average is higher (.364 to .337) than it was at the same time two years ago. Where he figures to cash in, however, is in the home-run and runs-batted-in departments.

With his two hits Sunday in the Royals' 7-2 victory over the Cleveland Indians, Brett raised his average to .364. His sixth inning home run—No. 17 on the year—drove in his 57th run. The power numbers are impressive considering his career bests—both accomplished in 1980—are 24 home runs and 118 RBIs.

"I know I'm way ahead of where I was in 1980," Brett said after hitting his third home run in the last six games. "I was hitting .330 or something about this time. The thing I don't try to do is compare everything to '80 because that year we had a tremendous lead—13, 14 games or whatever. You could be more of an individual because nobody was going to catch us. I can't think now or later about what my average is. We're in a situation where I've got to try and help the club win games."

Certainly, Brett couldn't be asked to do more of late to help the cause. An exception might be, of course, if he wanted to try his hand at pitching. But as a hitter, the All-Star third baseman has been on a torrid streak.

He brings an eight-game hitting streak (14 for 32) into tonight's nationally televised game with the Toronto Blue Jays in Toronto. Yet the most surprising facet is his development as a legitimate power hitter. Already this month he has five home runs. Of his 17 this year, 13 have come on the road.

"When I first came up I would have been happy with 10 (home runs)," Brett said. "Then I hit 15, then 20. I hit 21 last year. So, in spring training looking ahead, I'd be disappointed if I didn't hit 20.

"Now, it's 25 to 30. If my performance doesn't tail off, I should do that easy. I'm still going to hit for an average. That's why I'm happy so far. I look at (Rod) Carew with two (home runs) and (Wade) Boggs with one, and they're the top hitters."

Brett credits his power production to physical maturity and good old fundamentals. The swing remains the same. He isn't swinging for the fences or walking to the plate with the idea of swatting the ball out of the park.

"I'm a streaky hitter like everyone else," he said. "But when I'm not at the top of my game I still get hits. When I'm at the top of my game is when I really hit—a lot of home runs, a lot of extra-base hits.

"Right now, I'm swinging the bat as good as I ever have."

july 25, 1983

by Mike McKenzie

Umpires' Ruling Beats the Tar out of Royals

NEW YORK—George Brett laughed. The laughter turned instantly to rage. Rage gave over to tears. And tears of frustration and disbelief eventually dissolved into a dispassionate lull.

He touched all bases of a home run of emotions. All because of a home run of infamy.

Eventually, shower-drenched and with time to pacify his swirl of feelings, Brett stood before a world of questioners, shook his head, sighed and said, "If I had any guts I'd retire, because now I've seen it all."

What he had seen at approximately 4:40 p.m., Yankee Stadium time, was a Goose Gossage fastball rising high and far off his bat and into the right-field grandstand, apparently giving the Royals a 5-4 grip on a possible victory with two outs in the top half of the ninth inning.

Moments later he saw home-plate umpire Tim McClelland, after several minutes of confusion and commotion that included using home plate as a measuring rod, step toward the Royals' dugout and signal Brett out.

The third out. The game, therefore, was over. Two runs on Brett's homer did not count. The Yankees won 4-3.

The pine tar Brett had applied to his bat—to improve grip and prevent blisters, he said—extended highter on the barrel of the bat than the 18 inches allowed by the rules.

Yankees Manager Billy Martin had the umpires check the bat, at the behest of one of his coaches, Don Zimmer.

"I was in the dugout laughing at them," Brett said. "They had no case."

"We had nothing to measure with," umpire crew chief Joe Brinkman said later. He used the front edge of home plate, which is 17 inches across. Brinkman said the pine tar extended in thick substance a "good 19 to 20 inches" and in a lighter amount even higher.

Brett lost control when he was called out. He rushed from the dugout toward McClelland. Brett's cheeks puffed in and out, like bellows, as strong words and heavy breaths fought for space around his chew of tobacco. If ever there was a raging bull ...

And Brett's primary epithet of disbelief, witnessed through lip reading on television monitors and surely blistering to the umpires' ears, had something to do with bull. It wasn't feathers.

So, Brett had the ignominious distinction of hitting a game-losing home run, and Gossage got a save by giving up a hit into the seats.

Royals Manager Dick Howser telephoned the American League office to protest the umpires' decision, and today he will send a telegram formally lodging an appeal.

George Brett is restrained by umpire Joe Brinkman as Brett argues with umpire Tim McClelland, holding the bat at right, after McClelland called Brett out for having too much pine tar on his bat in a game at Yankee Stadium in New York on July 24, 1983. Four days later, the umpire's decision was reversed by the league and the last four outs of the game were played in a special game in August.

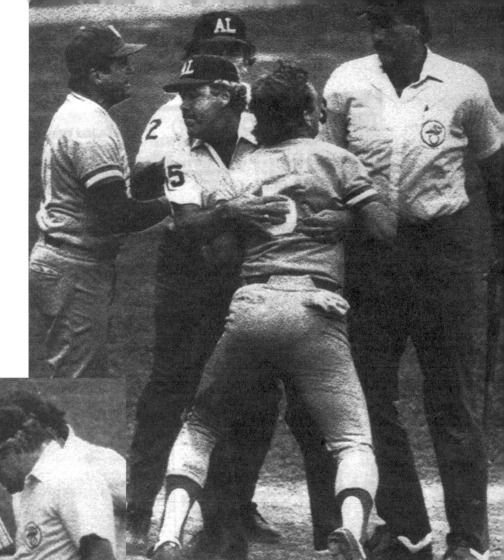

Robert Rodriguez, AP/Wide World Photos

Umpire Tim McClelland measures the pine tar on the handle of George Brett's bat as New York Yankees manager Billy Martin watches. McClelland's out call on Brett, for using too much tar on the bat came after Brett had homered in the ninth inning. Martin protested the bat to McClelland, setting off a huge argument.

july 28, 1983

by The Kansas City Star

It's a Homer, by George!

Well, the umpires didn't win this one.

American League President Lee MacPhail overruled the umpires today and ordered that George Brett's two-run homer against the New York Yankees last Sunday count, though it was hit with a bat which the umpires said was illegal beause of excessive pine tar.

It was the first time in MacPhail's 10-year tenure that he has overruled the umpires.

The Yankees had been declared 4-3 winners over the Royals when the umpires disallowed Brett's home run and recorded it instead as the final out.

Now, the game will be treated as a suspended game and must be completed, if practical. It would be resumed with two outs in the top of the ninth with the Royals leading 5-4. Because the Royals and Yankees are not scheduled to play each other the rest of the season, the game will be completed only if first place is at stake for either team, according to Bob Fishel, assistant to MacPhail.

"It could be the 18th (of August)," Fishel said. "It could be the day after the end of the season. It could never be played."

All records, including Brett's home run, will count, however.

Fishel said a decision would be made later on possible disciplinary action against Brett, who bumped an umpire in the uproar that followed the decision nullifying the home run.

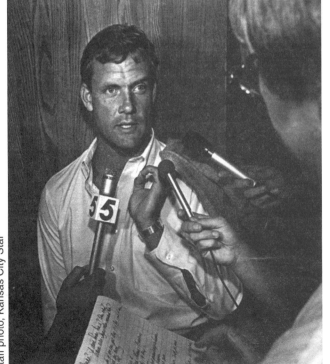

Royals third baseman George Brett talks with the news media at Kansas City International Airport after American League President Lee MacPhail overruled the umpires and reinstated Brett's two-run homer.

Staff photo, Kansas City Star

1983

by Dennis Dodd

Brett Hopes Pine-Tar Game Is Behind Him

The subject disgusts George Brett. Television sportscasters want a few profound words from him, expanding upon it. Reporters have tried to wrench it out of him with methods similar to an interrogation.

For the record, Royals third baseman George Brett said he doesn't want to talk about, be near or even refer to the pine-tarred bat that has caused him more grief these past 25 days than the rush-hour traffic on the Santa Monica Freeway, near his boyhood home in El Segundo, Calif. He would just as soon get back to his job. He appears to be emerging from his first extended slump of the season and is eager to put the past behind.

Brett still has the bat in limbo—just as the famous four-outs-remaining game with the New York Yankees was in the New York state court system until two hours before game time Thursday. State Supreme Court Justice Orest V. Maresca saw to that Thursday morning with his temporary injunction, supporting suits brought by fans who asked to be allowed in free to a game they claimed they had paid to see to conclusion on July 24. In the jumble of events that followed, an appellate justice overturned the ruling, and the Royals went on to win the nearly month-old game 5-4.

But Brett, the star of the overwrought show, was somewhere in the land of crabcakes and Spiro Agnew—not at a New York airport, not standing in the wings at Yankee Stadium. He was whisked off straight

Billy Martin, New York Yankee manager and protester of the famed pine tar bat, presents the Grace Under Pressure award to George Brett in December 1983.

to Baltimore, along with another ejectee from the July 24 fracas—pitcher Gaylord Perry.

"The Royals encouraged me not to be seen," Brett said. "There will be an avalanche of questions and an avalanche of reporters. I'd rather stay out of it. People are going to try to set up a duel between me and Billy Martin or George Steinbrenner. That's simply not true."

by Jack Etkin

Royals Can Only Recall What September Used to Be Like

Vendors still sell peanuts and beer, and the water does its between-innings dance in the fountains in right field. Outwardly everything seems in order at Royals Stadium.

Big-leaguers are playing September baseball, and the games should count more than ever. They don't. Not at all.

The baseball season in Kansas City has become a shell. Three remaining weeks of the schedule are some Hollywood set of buildings where the facade exists and nothing more. Nothing.

Elsewhere, hearts may flutter at this nightly ebb and flow because in other places the baseball still matters. Not here. Not in September.

The home team has lost 10 of its last 12 games. Kansas City has tried staying ahead of Texas and Oakland in the standings. The stakes are second, third or fourth place. Is the difference all that important?

The special tang of the pennant race is no more. No start-the-workday chitchat about the home team. Not this September. Not here.

Winning is not what's missing here. Look at last season. Didn't the Royals collapse in September? Being there—that is the crucial variable. That is the pennant race fun. That is the magic unfolding in other places.

Sign of '84? Brett to Play More at First

September 7, 1983
By Mike Fish

Call it a sign of the changing times. Or maybe a look into the future—as in next season.

What the Royals may have here is the arrival of their first baseman of the future—George Brett. In a not-too-surprising development, Manager Dick Howser has decided to shuffle Brett to first base for the final month of the season. That figures to park Willie Aikens even farther down the bench.

Tuesday night, Brett made his fifth start at first base this season as the Seattle Mariners defeated the Royals 3-1. Brett said after the game that Howser told him he'd play first base "60 to 70 percent of the time" this month.

"If they think I would be a better player over there, or help the team over there, I'd be happy to move," Brett said.

1983

We are all awed by his talents. I'm glad that when I'm 50 I'll be able to say I played with George Brett (above signing autographs for fans).

—Jamie Quirk,
Royals' catcher and one of Brett's close friends

An Injured Brett

After injuries forced him to miss the first 33 games of the 1984 season, Brett was eager to get back in the swing of things, literally. In his first game back, he went a perfect four for four. He was selected to the All-Star team, and his home run was the only run for the American League, who lost to the National League 3-1.

The famous "pine tar" incident was inescapable for Brett, and it seemed that everyone wanted to get their hands on the famous bat, including the Royals.

Just before the end of the season Brett again was injured. This time it was his hamstring, but he wasn't stopping for it. The Royals won the AL West and headed into the playoffs, where, despite Brett's heroics, they were defeated by the record-setting Detroit Tigers. Once the disappointment subsided, the team looked ahead with optimism. The Royals were right where they wanted to be.

may 19, 1984

by Tom Friend

Brett Zooms Off with Hitting Throttle Wide Open

1984

At 6:15 p.m. Friday, George Brett said he was through talking. Time to play ball, not speak it. Heaven knows, it was time to work on the game face.

It'd been a while.

But it didn't show. On the second pitch he saw this season, he lined a double to left field and scored the Royals' only run. On the third pitch, he lined a single to right. Then he walked. Then he singled again.

Batting average: 1.000.

Yes, Brett played baseball Friday night. He had been out for the first 33 games of the season because of ligament damage in his left knee. And it wasn't easy for him.

He said it's no fun not to play, period.

He said it's no fun to see your buddies up there leaving men on base when you know you can bring them home.

He said it's no fun waking up with a pain in the neck. And that happened because his pain in the knee made him toss and turn all night.

Being injured is tough. But that makes it so much more fun to come back.

"I like opening day," Brett said.

And that's why he decided to open his opening day early. It was 2:30 p.m., to be exact. He walked into the locker room—normally, he gets to the ballpark at 3 or 3:30—and he knew he was going to play. That's because the team doctors told him so.

But the doctors hadn't told the players. And that's why Brett's teammates played

reporter. At 3:35, rookies Mark Gubicza and Bret Saberhagen strolled into the clubhouse. Saberhagen saw Brett. He stared at Brett. He wanted to hear good news.

Saberhagen: "What's up?"

No answer from Brett. But his thumb pointed toward the ceiling. That said a lot.

Saberhagen: "What'd you find out?"

Brett likes the thumb routine. He did it again.

Saberhagen gave him a high four (Brett's thumb didn't make it).

Willie Wilson—who also was playing in his first home game since last year—interrupted Brett's important reading to ask an important question.

"Playing?" Wilson said.

Another thumb.

Yes, this was a thumbs-up night for Brett, even though the Royals lost 2-1. In his first at-bat in the first inning (his second pitch), he popped a Dave Stewart pitch into the left-field corner for a double. He scored on Hal McRae's bloop single to right.

In the third inning, he singled Pat Sheridan from first to third base, but the Royals couldn't score. In the fifth, Stewart got behind Brett 3-0, and, when Sheridan stole second, Brett was intentionally walked.

In the eighth, Brett singled again and was replaced by pinch runner Greg Pryor.

Instant impact.

But before the game he said he was wondering whether he'd be an instant flop.

"I had doubts about everything," he said after the game. "I've never concentrated so much in my life to be honest with you. I thought I concentrated during the World Series and every year in the playoffs, but tonight in the second inning, I was mentally drained … physically and mentally….

"And it was one of the few nights when I wished everybody would hit me a ground ball …So I usually say: 'Don't hit it to me. I want to enjoy the ballgame.' But tonight I said: 'Hey, let me do it.'

"I couldn't believe some of the things I was saying between pitches. I was into the game so much …I was scared to death when I was driving to the ballpark. I said: 'What will they do? Laugh at me? Boo me because I signed a long-term contract and everybody thinks I'm greedy?'

"After all that worrying …"

He had visited Dr. Steve Joyce on Thursday and knew he might play. But he said he wasn't sure.

Brett's legs were strong, stronger than they were a year ago.

So now where would he play? Royals Manager Dick Howser and Brett talked about it. He could have been the designated hitter, but Howser said he liked McRae there. He could have been in the outfield, but Howser said he already had enough outfielders.

So Brett was to play third base, batting third, Brett said fine. He just wanted to open his opening day.

But there were still more worries. He had to wear this newfangled knee brace that the Royals' trainers had found in a catalogue. Brett said he'd never worn one of them before.

And then there was his fielding. He'd taken some fielding practice a couple of

times but had never moved much.

"It's just like riding a bike," Saberhagen said. "You never forget."

Brett made his thumb point downward.

"I ran hard, but I don't know about my speed," he said. "I ran hard during my workouts, but I wasn't going anywhere."

He also said he just didn't want to get hurt again.

"I've got to make sure I don't pull a muscle or something," he said. "That'll be embarrassing."

Saberhagen: "What about hemorrhoids?"

Brett: "That'll be embarrassing. God just wanted me to have hemorrhoids."

And what about Brett's hitting?

"Off the coaches, my timing was fine," Brett said. "But (Rangers starter) Dave Stewart throws gas. The people down the left-field line better get gloves. I'll be a little late. I've had enough batting practice where I should be ready. I just hope I'll be around to put my uniform on tomorrow."

After missing the first 33 games of the 1984 season with a knee injury, Brett came back swinging and hit 1.000 on his "opening day."

Erik Hill, Kansas City Star

by Tracy Ringolsby

AL Strikes Out in Bid for Second Straight

Brett Homers

George Brett and the AL team were defeated by the NL team for the 20th time in 22 games in the 1984 All-Star Game.

SAN FRANCISCO—They talked about the winds of Candlestick Park for weeks before they took the field Tuesday night for the 56th version of the All-Star Game.

A breezy night it was, as the National League regained the winning touch with a 3-1 victory over the American League in front of a crowd of 57,796, a Candlestick Park record. It was the National League's 20th victory in the last 22 games.

Royals third baseman George Brett provided the lone American League run with a home run in the second inning. But the National League got an unearned run in the first inning and bases-empty home runs from Montreal catcher Gary Carter in the second and Atlanta outfielder Dale Murphy in the eighth inning in improving its All-Star record to 36-19-1.

Call It a Sticky Deal

So you want to bargain, do you?

Well George Brett apparently is adept at recognizing a good deal when he sees one.

You may recall Brett negotiated a "lifetime" contract with Royals co-owner Avron Fogelman this spring. Big bucks, right?

All Brett was asked to do was go about his baseball business for the next decade or so. But Fogelman wasn't done dealing. His final demand was for Brett to get his hands on the celebrated pine-tar bat so it could be put on display at Royals Stadium.

That was accomplished recently when New Jersey sports collector Barry Halper graciously returned the bat. Brett had given the bat to Halper, a friend and limited partner in the New York Yankees, after the controversial game last summer at Yankee Stadium.

"Mr. Fogelman mentioned in the negotiations how he would like to have the bat back," Brett said. "It was a friendly statement. I mean, here was a guy who had gone out on the limb for me. The least I could do was go out on a limb and get it back for him."

According to Brett, the bat is in Fogelman's possession.

"It wasn't me personally asking George," said Fogelman, who also is a collector of baseball memorabilia. "I was representing the Royals in the conversation. We felt the bat should be here."

Brett said Halper was very understanding when Brett told him of his predicament last spring.

For his part, Brett offered Halper the bat he used in hitting three homers off Catfish Hunter during a 1978 playoff game.

"We also don't know just when, but at some time we're gong to loan the bat to the Hall of Fame to display."

Brett displays the bat he used to hit the famous "pine tar" home run.

1984

by Tracy Ringolsby

No Time to Hurt—
Brett Just Wants To Play

ANAHEIM, Calif.—This American League West race doesn't allow anybody to nestle into a comfort zone. The Royals went into Tuesday night's game against the California Angels sitting atop the AL West, leading both the Angels and the Minnesota Twins, who lost 5-3 to Chicago on Tuesday night, by $1\frac{1}{2}$ games.

No time for relaxation. No time for sitting back. No time, Royals third baseman George Brett said, for healing—at least not fully.

Brett started at third base for the Royals on Tuesday, his second start in a row but only his third start since suffering a torn left hamstring in Boston on August 30. Brett started in last Wednesday's 3-2 victory in Minnesota but missed the weekend series in Seattle before returning to play in Monday's 10-1 victory over the Angels.

He's better but not at his best.

"I think it is fair to say I'm limited right now," Brett said of his ability to play. "When I try to accelerate, I can feel it. It bothers me."

It does not, however, bother him as much as not playing at all. The Royals are in a race, and Brett said the worst feeling of all is to not be in the lineup.

"If we were 20 games up or out, it wouldn't be that important," Brett said. "If we were 30 up, Dick (Howser, Royals manager) would say, 'Take it easy and get ready for the playoffs and World Series.' For us, this is the playoffs and World Series. This is what the season is all about."

So Brett comes in the park early each afternoon, around 2 p.m., for a special therapy session with trainer Mickey Cobb. There's a stretching routine. There's a rubdown. There's running in the outfield. And on days such as Tuesday, when the Royals had early batting practice, there are a few extra swings of the bat.

Through it all remains a fear that with one quick movement Brett will be back on the bench because of a new tear in the hamstring.

"I have it controlled when I hit," Brett said. "I can keep telling myself I'm not going to run hard, I'm not going to stretch a single into a double, I'm not going to break up double plays.

"(However,) when I get in the field …defense is reactions. You can't control that. I didn't have to go to my left or right for any balls on Monday. With defense, I won't know what is going to happen until it happens." Howser is trying to control things as much as possible; he said Brett might never fully recover from the injury before the season ends.

He plans to start him but get him out in the middle innings if possible, as in Monday's victory over the Angels. With the Royals leading 5-0 in the top of the fifth, Greg Pryor came in to run after Brett walked with one out.

"We have to play every game right now like it is a playoff game," Howser said. "He's part of us winning. I want to get George in, hope he can produce in the early or middle part of the game and then get him out." The Royals are hoping that Brett can bounce back from this injury in the style he has shown before. Nine previous times Brett has been sidelined by injury for nine or more games. In the first nine games back each time—a total of 81 games—he has a career .342 in batting average.

Monday, he was hitless in two at-bats before waiting. He sliced a fly ball to left in the first inning and then lined out to first baseman Daryl Sconiers leading off the fourth.

"I hit that one right on the bench," Brett said. "It was a nice swing, a nice feeling."

Right now, Brett said he's not worrying about getting rest or reinjuring the hamstring. Each of the last two days, Brett said he has felt better than the day before.

"The doctor said if I feel a sting when I move, that's no good," Brett said. "There was a pretty constant stinging, but I don't get that stinging right now except when I try to run real fast. Mickey said the flexibility in my leg is as good right now as it has been all year long."

Royals Are Disappointed They Lost, but Next Year Is Another Day

October 6, 1984
By Joe McGuff

DETROIT—This is the time of year when the baseball season is at its peak, when the highs are so high and the lows are so low.

Seven days after experiencing the euphoria of winning the American League West, the Royals were choking on the disappointment of three straight losses to the Detroit Tigers in the AL playoffs.

In general the mood in the Kansas City clubhouse was one of disappointment, but not desolation. They were taking pride in how far they had come and looking forward to even better things next year.

"I think it was a great year," Royals reliever Dan Quisenberry said.

George Brett also took a positive view.

"I think the front office has got to be pleased with the season. We're a good hitting club, but we faced three of the top pitchers in the American League in this series."

"What a masterpiece Charlie Leibrandt pitched. I don't think they hit a ball hard. It's amazing to think he'd give up one run here and lose because this is a hitter's park."

**Being down and out as much as we were and accomplishing what we did is unbelievable. I've been on some great ballclubs in the '70s. This year we were a great ballclub, but this year was a little different. This was a great ballclub inside.
—George Brett on the 1985 Royals**

George Brett set the pace for his team in the 1985 season. For the first time in his career, Brett was the top vote-getter among AL All-Stars, extending his streak as the top vote-getter at third base for the 10th consecutive year.

The Royals won the AL West and advanced to play Toronto for the pennant. Down two games to none, Brett pulled his team out of the fire with a phenomenal performance in game three. After hitting two home runs and a double, Brett singled in the eighth and scored the game-winning run. The Royals went on to win the series 4-3.

In only their second World Series appearance, the Royals beat the St. Louis Cardinals in yet another comeback performance. The "I-70 Series" became etched forever in baseball lore when the Royals rallied in the ninth inning and won game six, aided by a controversial call from first-base umpire Don Denkinger. With the series leveled at three games apiece, the Royals exploded for an 11-0 victory in game seven—igniting championship celebrations throughout Kansas City. The season was capped off for Brett when he was later awarded the Gold Glove for being the best-fielding third baseman in the league in 1985.

by Randy Covitz

Brett Keeps Hitting, Royals Keep Winning

It's a mystery to George Brett. He calls Chicago's Britt Burns one of the toughest left-handers around.

"But I hit him," Brett said after driving in four runs in the Royals' 8-4 victory Friday night over the White Sox.

Of course, Brett has been hitting most everyone lately. And, with Willie Wilson and Lonnie Smith dashing around the bases, Brett's hits keep turning into runs batted in.

He's driven in 10 runs in the last four games, including two four-RBI games in the last three outings. Wilson and Smith have scored eight of those runs, and Brett accounted for the two others on home runs.

"That's what happens when guys get on base; you can drive in some runs," said Brett, who drove in all four runners that were on ahead of him.

Brett, who had two singles against Burns and one against another left-hander, Juan Agosto, didn't get a chance in the eighth, when White Sox right-hander Gene Nelson walked him intentionally with a runner at second and two outs. But Steve Balboni singled in the final run of the game, and the Royals won their third straight, their ninth in the last 12 games and moved into second place in the Western Division, 1 $\frac{1}{2}$ games behind California.

Sandman Pays Visit to Royals' Bat Rack

Mike Fish
June 12, 1985

OAKLAND, Calif.—Keep the noise to a hush, please. The Royals' bats are taking one of their periodic snoozes. Just a quiet breather.

A few games here, a few there. Same old story: few hits and fewer runs. All of which leads to a few losses—three straight, to be exact.

The Royals have scored four runs in their last three games. And George Brett hasn't started a game since last Friday.

Down with a pulled right hamstring muscle, Brett probably won't return to the starting lineup until at least this weekend in Seattle. Great news to the A's. Even greater news for their manager, Jackie Moore.

"It's a lot easier without him (Brett)," Moore said. "Any time you can get through a series without seeing him it's nice."

by Jonathan Rand

Brett Deserves His Status

George Brett was sitting in front of his cubicle late Friday afternoon, thumbing through the sports pages, and couldn't help but notice his name was conspicuous on two lists. Among American League vote-getters for the All-Star Game, his 909,433 votes led not only third basemen, but everybody else, too. Among American League batters, only Rickey Henderson of the New York Yankees, hitting .352, led Brett, hitting .343.

The main difference between those lists is that Brett still would be prominent in the balloting were he hitting .240.

"Popularity is all the game is," said Brett, a household name in baseball who will win the AL All-Star balloting at third base for the 10th consecutive year.

"Right now, I deserve to be the starting third baseman, but there were years I didn't deserve it.

"What is it that makes me popular?

"Is it doing endorsements on television? It is hitting .390 in 1980? Is it hitting a home run against (Goose) Gossage (that put the Royals in the 1980 World Series)? Is it the pine-tar incident? I've been in the center of a little controversy, had some success and had

some failures. I've gotten some big hits in big games, but it's hard to pinpoint what makes me more popular than other players."

Being on the other list, though, has nothing to do with compliments. Ranking among the batting leaders has nothing to do with what you did in 1980 or on a razor commercial. Batting averages, unlike compliments, aren't given to just anybody.

Rob Kozloff, AP/Wide World Photos

George Brett, Wade Boggs, and Eddie Murray share a laugh during batting practice at the All-Star Game in Minneapolis.

1985

by Joe McGuff

Brett Puts His Stamp on AL Playoff Series

I f you weren't there Friday night for game three of the American League Championship Series, you should have been. If you were there, you saw a performance that will become a part of baseball's postseason lore along with Don Larsen's perfect World Series game, Babe Ruth's called-shot home run and Reggie Jackson's three home runs in the sixth game of the 1977 Series.

There are rare and wonderful moments when a great athlete throws aside the restraints that his humanity places on him and plays at a level that fills us with joy and awe. Friday night was one of those occasions.

Perhaps never has one player so dominated a big game as George Brett did. The Royals were gasping for life in their playoff series with Toronto. They had lost the first two games and were at risk of losing their 11th straight game in postseason play.

Brett hit a home run over the right-field fence in the first inning. He hit a double that was two feet from the top of the right-field wall in the fourth. He hit a home run to deep left-center in the sixth. In the eighth, he singled and scored the winning run.

He also executed a defensive play in the genre of Brooks Robinson's vacuum-cleaner performance in the 1970 World Series. In the third inning Brett made a backhand stop of Lloyd Moseby's sharply hit ball down the third-base line, leaped and threw across his

body to retire the fleet Damaso Garcia, who attempted to score from third.

Saturday night the Royals lost to the Blue Jays 3-1 and trail in the series three games to one, but in years to come the series between the Royals and the Blue Jays will be remembered not so much for who won or lost, but because of what Brett did in the third game. It was a performance that makes the spirit soar and creates the sort of excitement that is renewable every time the sights and sounds of this night come to mind.

Big games in postseason play are nothing new for Brett, but the totality of his performance in such a desperate situation goes beyond anything he has done before.

"We are awed by his talents," said Jamie Quirk, the Royals' reserve catcher and one of Brett's close friends. "When I came up to him after the game, I told him, 'I don't know what to say. You are unbelievable.' I'm glad that when I'm 50 I'll be able to say I played with George Brett."

John Wathan, shaking his head in wonderment, recalled a scene on the bench in the sixth.

"When George came up," Wathan related, "Jamie said, 'If he hits a home run, I'll take my clothes off and run on the field naked.' Jamie didn't do it, but I had his top two buttons off. Every time there is a big game, George is phenomenal."

1985

by Tracy Ringolsby

Quite a Royal Comeback, Eh?

KC Wins 3rd Straight for Pennant

TORONTO—They had been scoffed at for their lack of offense, buried more than once in recent months and kidded about the competition in their division.

But Wednesday night, the Royals beat the Toronto Blue Jays 6-2, winning the second American League pennant in their 17-year history. Their offense came alive, pulling them out of a postseason grave and gaining some respect for the AL West.

"The critics said we were in the weakest division," Royals Manager Dick Howser said. "We proved we could play in the East (50-34 in the regular season). We beat the best club in the East, the Toronto Blue Jays."

The Royals, who would have been eliminated in the best-of-five format that existed until this year, are only the fifth AL West Club to reach the World Series since the inception of division play in 1969.

1985

Brett leads the cheering from the dugout as the Royals led the Blue Jays 6-1 in the seventh game of the AL playoffs.

by **The Kansas City Star**

Royals Champs Of Missouri—and World

11-0 Victory Caps Historic Comeback

T hey did it!

By George, they did it!

The Royals are the world champions—and it wasn't even close. The Royals tore into the St. Louis Cardinals for an 11-0 victory Sunday night in the seventh game of the World Series, capping a historic comeback in Royals Stadium.

In fact, the Cardinals came completely unraveled. With the Royals building their lead to 11-0 with a six-run fifth inning, both St. Louis Manager Whitey Herzog and pitcher Joaquin Andujar were ejected from the game for arguing with home-plate umpire Don Denkinger. Andujar had to be forcibly removed by his teammates.

By then the Cardinals already knew they had blown their once formidable 3-1 World Series lead. By then the Cardinals knew they would go down in history as the only team ever to lose a World Series after winning the first two games on the road. By then it was clear which clubhouse President Reagan would be calling Sunday night. By then it was over.

There's no doubt about it, they DID IT!

OK, now think back—and be honest. When did you first give up hope—or at least have a little lapse in confidence—for this bunch of Royals?

Was it in July when the Royals fell 7 $\frac{1}{2}$ games behind in the American League West race?

How about in September when the Royals let a three-game lead slip away, fueled when Seattle swept a four-game series?

Or was it when California dropped the Royals a game behind by winning the second game of a four-game series in Kansas City?

How about when Toronto built a 3-1 lead in the American League Championship Series or when the Royals headed to Toronto for the last two games of the playoffs trailing three games to two?

Did you think it was over when the Cardinals shockingly scored four runs in the ninth inning, beating the Royals 4-2 for a lead of two games to none in the World Series?

Maybe when the Cardinals won the fourth game for a 3-1 World Series lead with the fifth game scheduled for Busch Stadium in St. Louis?

Well, the Royals didn't give up.

Never.

October 28, 1985

When thousands rushed the field after the game, the first duty of police officers there was to protect the players, said Capt. J.J. Harris of the Kansas City Police Department.

Second priority: protect the turf.

"The Royals just spent $2 million (before the beginning of the season) on a new field," Capt. Harris said. "It's our job to protect the carpet."

Staff photo, Kansas City Star

B ret Saberhagen receives a hug from George Brett after winning the World Series.

by Jeff Taylor

Hail, the Conquering Royals

Thousands Swarm to Downtown

1985

In the heart of Kansas City, it was a delirious and sometimes dangerous afternoon of celebration Monday—a day of frenzy on Grand Avenue as a wide blue river of fans paid homage to their World Champion Royals.

Above all, it was a day of history and good memories, a time for thousands of baseball fans near and far—from the very young to the very old—to toss aside the humdrum of work and school, to play hooky from their obligations.

It was party time.

But not all was good. In the thick of a parade along Grand Avenue—where about 225,000 fans lined the curbs—and a rally at the Liberty Memorial Mall, there were car fires and wrecks and fights over confetti. There were problems for police in contending with the huge crowds and the traffic, and problems with the planning that went into it all.

Even so, the celebration was a steady current of enthusiasm and streamers and balloons and car horns. All through downtown, heaps of confetti and shredded paper lay strewn across the roads and curbs like freshly cut hay in a field.

For the first time in 17 seasons, the Royals had claimed it all. And on the day after, Royals followers came by the thousands to get glimpses of the princes of the city.

By midafternoon, the spotlight narrowed to the Liberty Memorial Mall, where a throng of 125,000 sign-toting, pennant-waving fans had gathered since late morning for a rally to honor the Royals.

At 1:30 p.m., the first of the Royals—littered with confetti—squeezed onto the speaker's platform. In front of them, thousands of fans, already packed scores deep, pushed tighter and tighter toward the temporary stage to steal a glimpse of the players.

At the Liberty Memorial, it all began in the late morning when the first fans filtered onto the mall. By noon, a mob of 30,000 had gathered, Kansas City Police Capt. Dave Bremson said.

By 2:10 p.m., the crowd, more than double the capacity of Royals Stadium, got a chance to see what it wanted: the team.

Royals President Joe Burke got the masses hopping as he gyrated to the team's theme song. George Brett earned the largest applause as he thanked the crowd for its support.

Thousands of fans swarmed Grand Avenue in Kansas City to thank their World Champion Royals.

by Tracy Ringolsby

Gold Glove Shows Brett Scooped Up Some Believers

George Brett says he is going to put the Gold Glove he was awarded Tuesday next to the hat from the Pine Tar Game in his family's Manhattan Beach, Calif., restaurant.

"We'll call it the Ripley's Believe It or Not Department," Brett said.

Two years after Brett approached the Royals about moving from third base to another position, American League managers and coaches voted him the best-fielding third baseman in the league in 1985.

Brett was selected on 19 of the 77 ballots for the award given annually by *The Sporting News*. Brook Jacoby of Cleveland was second with 16 votes, Wade Boggs of Boston and Jim Presley of Seattle tied for third with 10 votes, and Doug DeCinces of California had nine.

Certainly, the trade of Buddy Bell from Texas to Cincinnati in the middle of the 1985 season played a part in Brett's selection. Bell won the award for third basemen the six previous seasons.

"He definitely had a good reputation, the best in the American League," Brett said of Bell. "With players like Buddy and Graig Nettles (now with San Diego), they are known as defensive players who can hit a little. I was an offensive player who could field a little.

"When people talked about me, they always talked hitting. After this season, I can be counted as a complete baseball player, not just an offensive player."

Brett said he thought his efforts in 1985 were his all-time best. He hit .335, had 112 runs batted in and hit a career-high 30 home runs. Defensively, Brett led AL third basemen in assists with 339 and double plays with 33.

Brett made only 15 errors in 461 chances, and his .967 fielding percentage ranked second among AL third basemen who appeared in at least 100 games. Rance Mulliniks, who platooned at third base in Toronto, had a .971 percentage.

"Two months ago, a friend told me not to get my hopes up about winning the MVP, but he said I had a good chance to win the Gold Glove," Brett said. "I just laughed. With third basemen like Boggs and DeCinces, there's still some tough competition, but none of us had a name for ourselves defensively like Buddy.

"I didn't want to get my hopes up, but I thought I had a good enough year to deserve it. I thought I had a good enough year for the MVP, too, but … ."

Brett finished second in AL MVP voting to Don Mattingly of the New York Yankees. Both Brett, who won AL MVP honors in 1980, and Mattingly, a first baseman, were Gold Glove winners.

"This is something I never thought I could win," Brett said. "I didn't have much confidence in my ability to play the position (two years ago when he asked to move to first base or left field).

1985

Keith Myers, Kansas City Star

George Brett's play at third base earned him a Gold Glove in 1985.

AP/Wide World Photos

Vice President George Bush talks with members of the World Champion Royals at the White House. From left: Royals manager Dick Howser, Bret Saberhagen, Bush, and George Brett.

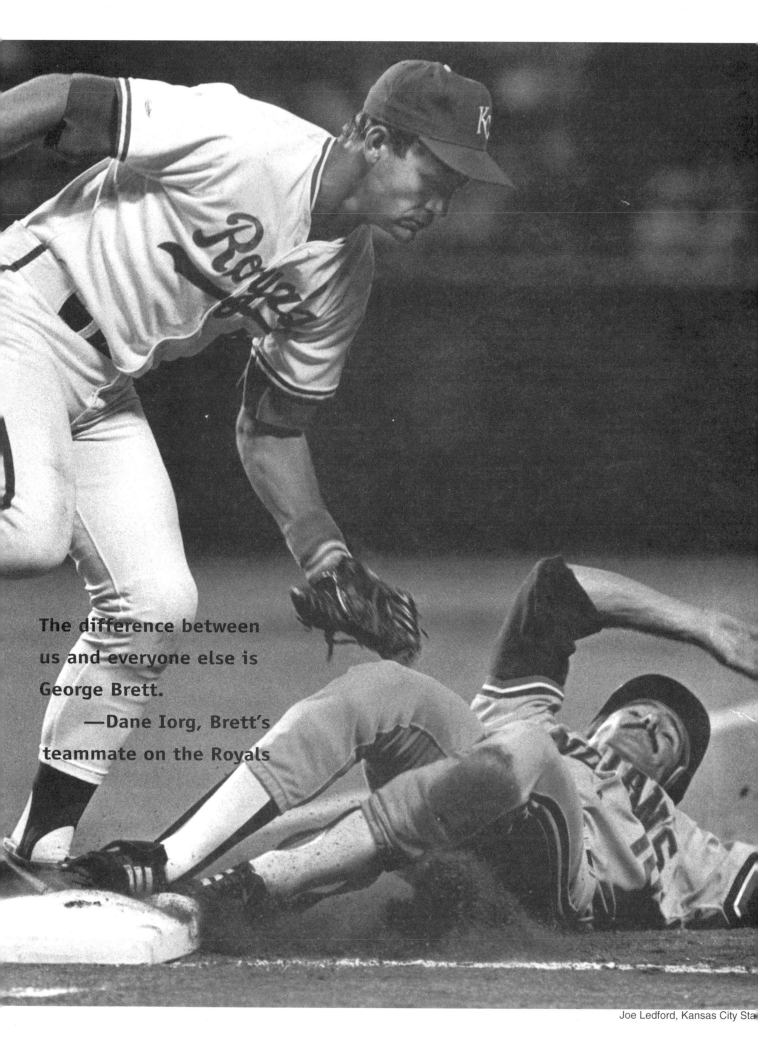

The difference between us and everyone else is George Brett.

—Dane Iorg, Brett's teammate on the Royals

A Year for the Record Books

Coming off the championship 1985 season, it might have seemed as if things were at their best for George Brett. But he wasn't satisfied.

Motivated by his father's skepticism, Brett started fast in 1986, setting Royals club records for career home runs at 195 and all-time RBIs at 993. In May, Brett achieved what he considered to be his greatest career milestone of 2,000 hits. His 1,000th RBI and 200th career home run came on the same ball in June, making him one of only eight active major-leaguers to reach both milestones.

The record-setting pace Brett was travelling at came to a screeching halt with yet another injury, this time to Brett's shoulder. Though he was selected to his 11th consecutive All-Star team, he was unable to play in that game or in the last 38 games of the season. The Royals finished the season out of contention, and Brett had successful shoulder surgery in November.

by Jack Etkin

Royals Strike Back, Win One for Tradition

Brett Sets One for the Record

NEW YORK—With the strong weight of history behind them Wednesday, the Royals beat the New York Yankees 7-4.

Since the inception of the franchise in 1969, the Royals have not lost two games in a row at the outset of the season. They kept that proud streak intact by unleashing an offense that was virtually absent in their season-opening 4-2 defeat.

George Brett led the way with two home runs—both off the right-field foul pole—giving him a Royals career record of 195. He had been in a tie with Amos Otis, who hit 193 home runs while playing 14 seasons for the Royals. It was the eighth regular-season game in which Brett has hit two home runs and the first time he has done it against the Yankees. Brett has hit 12 regular-season home runs in Yankee Stadium and an additional five in the American League playoffs.

"I feel comfortable hitting here," Brett said. "Sometimes you have gray slacks or a favorite shirt. I just feel very comfortable when I stand in that batter's box and look out there. It's hard to explain what happens."

Brett Alone at Top

George Brett's two home runs on April 9, 1986, enabled him to break a tie with Amos Otis as the Royals' all-time home-run leader.

	Years as Royal	Homers as Royal
George Brett	**1973-present**	**195**
Amos Otis	1970-1983	193
Hal McRae	1973-present	162
John Mayberry	1972-1977	143
Frank White	1973-present	109

1986

may 15, 1986

by Bob Nightengale

Three-Hit Shutout Makes Gubicza's Night Complete

Brett Moves to Top of RBI List

This time there were handshakes thrust at him instead of condolences. This time, there was a cold bottle of champagne awaiting his celebration instead of warm beer to drown his sorrows. This time, Royals pitcher Mark Gubicza was a winner.

Completing perhaps the finest performance of his major-league career Wednesday night, Gubicza threw a three-hit shutout and defeated the Cleveland Indians 5-0 for his first victory of the season.

Just as important as Gubicza's numbers were the numbers compiled by George Brett, whose three runs batted in moved him to the top of the Royals' all-time RBI list and provided Gubicza with enough support.

Royals' Career RBI leaders (as of 5/14/86)

George Brett's three runs batted in on May 14, 1986, sent him past Amos Otis into the top spot on the Royals' all-time RBI list.

Player	RBIs
George Brett	993
Amos Otis	992
Hal McRae	980
Frank White	624
John Mayberry	552

may 26, 1986

by Jack Etkin

Brett Takes Final Step to 2,000 Hits

History appeared early in the afternoon, 13 innings from the game's end as it turned out. George Brett lined a fourth-inning single into right field and finally had career hit No. 2,000.

"That hit made it worthwhile," said Brett, who was one for seven in the Royals' 2-1 victory Sunday over the Chicago White Sox in 17 innings, "but it was a long day. It's a day I'll always remember and probably a day I'll try to forget as quick as possible."

Brett's single came on a 1-0 pitch from White Sox starter Joel Davis. Center fielder John Cangelosi threw the ball to shortstop Ozzie Guilllen, who ran over and flipped the keepsake to Brett at first base.

Brett called the hit "the biggest thrill I've had in a regular season. It's the biggest hit of my career because it is somewhat of a milestone to get 2,000."

He had not ticked off the hits in his mind, knowing that this single meant he needed six more and that double reduced his magic number to five on his way to 2,000.

He was trying not to think about milestones, knowing that to focus on hit No. 2,000 might prolong the entire process and send him into some hitless tailspin. Try as he might, though, that retrogression did occur.

"Now I can relax," said Brett, who became the 158th player in major-league history to collect 2,000 hits. "I think I might have been pressing a tad. I thought I was going to get it in Texas."

Getting 2,000 hits was once an equally far-fetched notion for Brett. Hurdles have appeared, and hurdles have been crossed. And 13 years in the big leagues have rolled by.

"I thought in all honesty that 1,000 was a lot," Brett said, "because in my first year of playing I didn't think I would be up in the major leagues very long. I wasn't an overnight success in the major leagues. I wasn't a star or very successful in the minor leagues.

"Charley (Lau) and I started working together, and things started happening, and I got my 1,000th hit, and it was a big thrill. Five hundred wasn't that big a deal, but 1,000 was. Fifteen hundred wasn't anything. It was a number."

Now there is another number. A bigger, rounder number. Brett has a makeshift plan for where the treasured baseball will go. He will put it with baseballs he has that have been signed by Bob Hope, Richard Nixon, Gerald Ford, Tom Watson, Brooks Robinson, Carl Yastrzemski and Pete Rose. He will put this baseball with other baseballs from other meaningful moments.

"I've got about 100 balls, and they're all in a trash can in my house," Brett said. "I've got a football from Joe Namath. And I've got all these things in a trash can. And it's going to go right in that trash can until I have a place that I can display them in my house."

june 2, 1986

by Rick Gosselin

Homer Allows Brett to Put Two More Milestones in the Can

A week ago Sunday George Brett tossed the baseball commemorating his 2,000th career hit into a trash can at his home that contains other memorabilia. He made another deposit Sunday.

This time it was the ball he hit for both his 200th career home run and his 1,000th RBI, a leadoff homer in the eighth off Mitch Williams onto the grassy area beyond the center-field wall for the final run in a 5-3 victory over the Texas Rangers.

Cliff Shiappa, AP/Wide World Photos

George Brett tips his helmet to the crowd after getting his 2,000th hit.

The Club

George Brett is one of only eight active major leaguers to have attained 2,000 hits, 1,000 runs batted in and 200 home runs in a career.

	Yrs.	HR	Hits	RBI
Tony Perez	23	377	2.686	1,625
Reggie Jackson	20	537	2,447	1,619
Graig Nettles	20	375	2,118	1,232
Ted Simmons	19	238	2,380	1,331
Steve Garvey	18	260	2,489	1,242
Cecil Cooper	16	228	2,031	1,046
Jim Rice	13	336	2,026	1,216
George Brett	**14**	**200**	**2,007**	**1,000**

One day all those balls will mean something to Brett. But not right now.

"It wouldn't mean anything," Brett said, "except that people kept coming up to me and saying, 'You've got 199 home runs,' and, 'You've got 999 RBIs.' It makes you feel like you've been playing forever."

by Kent Pulliam

Brett's 'Trash' a Storehouse of a Lifetime of Memories

Close your eyes to another time, another place. Envision the same stoop shouldered walk on another man. As George Brett tosses the football with Joe Namath's autograph on it from one hand to the other, you see him walking to the line of scrimmage and tossing a game-winning touchdown pass.

"George Toma got me this ball," Brett said of the groundskeeper at Royals Stadium. "The football has always been a favorite because I liked Joe Namath so much—except I can't read the inscription any more. I used to know what it said."

If it is a more familiar than special moment for George Brett, a short stroll through his collection of sports memorabilia is still a treat. Since 1982, these links to career highlights and sidelights have been at home in a trash can Brett received as a birthday present. The donor of the can has faded from memory. Some of the memories have faded as well for this man who popularized pine tar, blasted the Royals into their first World Series with a home run against Goose Gossage in the 1980 American League playoffs and seemingly is running into Baseball's Hall of Fame.

Sadaharu Oh, faded; Danny Kaye; Huey Lewis; 200th hit; Stevie O'Bradovich; Jerry Ford; Richard Nixon; Ralph Garr; last out at Metropolitan Stadium in Bloomington, Minn.; Rocky Colavito; Bobby Floyd; Carl Yastrzemski; Mickey Stanley; Bob Hope; 500th hit; Richie Hebner; Leslie something or other; Laurie Nixon, Miss Florida National Teenager; Victoria Principal, Linda Gray, Patrick Duffy and Larry Hagman of Dallas; Ronald Reagan …

But sifting through it all, the memories rise again, as brilliant as the colors of the painting of Babe Ruth that hangs in Brett's den.

"That bat?" Brett asks, pointing to the bat he used to hit the playoff homer against Gossage. "That one's legal (no pine tar).

"The painting is from the original Babe Ruth postage stamp. I knew the guy (Mark English) who was commissioned to do it. He drew me the picture for my birthday present."

In some respects Brett is no different from the fans who flock to the rows of seats behind the Royals' dugout during every home stand. He likes an autographed baseball as well as the next guy. He just has a better opportunity to collect them than most.

"I don't really have any special memories of some of them because I didn't get a lot of them," Brett said. "I didn't get the Joe DiMaggio, somebody gave it to me."

But the ball bearing Carl Yastrzemski's name is special.

"Maybe Yaz is (special) because I played against him and he was a boyhood idol of mine," Brett said. "When I was younger I tried to imitate his batting stance and things like that. In high school it worked. But in the minors I never hit .300. When I got to the major leagues I know I made a drastic change."

GEORGE BRETT
Essay by Joe Posnanski

People remember such small things about George Brett. The way he wore his hat. The way he hit off a tee. The way he swung his bat. There's nothing particularly grand in the way people reminisce about Brett. People may remember Mickey Mantle for his gargantuan home runs, they might recall Willie Mays making those dazzling catches, they can close their eyes and still see Pete Rose diving headfirst into third base. With Brett, though, it's different. People remember the dirt on his uniform. It's more personal, somehow.

He had such a regal career. He is the only player to gather 3,000 hits, 300 home runs, 600 doubles, 100 triples and 200 stolen bases in one lifetime, a numbers buffet. Surely, he was the greatest pure hitter of his generation. He won batting titles in three decades, his first as a cocky surfer dude of the 1970s. His second was unforgettable; he chased after .400 when he was at his apex, when he was the genius student of the guru Charley Lau, when it seemed no one could throw a fastball past him. He won his third in 1990, when he was 37 and supposedly past his prime, when everyone said he had lost his legs. He looked just fine. He whacked a league-leading 45 doubles that season to boot.

Staff Photo, The Kansas City Star

Brett collected more than 3,000 hits and 300 home runs and won three batting titles in his career.

John Sleezer, The Kansas City Star

Mostly, though, he hit baseballs when it mattered, when the spotlight shined, in crowded ballparks. That's his baseball legacy. He hit .373 in his two World Series. The New York Yankees feared him, for good reason, because Brett despised them and loved pounding the ball at Yankee Stadium. He hit three home runs off Catfish Hunter in one playoff game, smashed a long home run off Goose Gossage, the one that sent the Royals to their first World Series. In his most renowned performance, a 1985 playoff game against Toronto when the Royals were

Brett waves to the crowd during ceremonies honoring the 1985 world champion Royals.

on the brink of extinction, he hit two home runs, crushed a double, scored four runs and made a diving catch. The Royals won the World Series that season, of course, and when that game ended, the eminent Joe McGuff would write, simply, that "there are rare and wonderful moments when a great athlete throws aside the restraints that his humanity places on him and plays at a level that fills us with joy and awe."

So, with all of that, and the pine-tar home run, and the hemorrhoid attack during the 1980 World Series, and the sheer respect that opponents held for him—no player in American League history has been intentionally walked as often—you would think people would remember majestic things about Brett, they would remember the biggest home runs, the most important hits, the greatest plays, but no, mostly, they remember the look that Brett gave them once. They remember the way he crouched in the batter's box. They remember the way he pounded his glove, like a school kid, as he stood at third base. They remember the way he kissed home plate after his final game at Royals Stadium. They remember how hard he hugged Bret Saberhagen after the Royals won the World Series.

Here's a story. It was 1985, and a man went to coach an 8-year-old tee-ball team in Kansas City. He showed up and gathered all the little boys for batting practice. The first boy put the bat on his left shoulder and tried

to yank it around.

"Son," the coach asked, "are you left-handed?"

"No," the boy said.

"Well, then, you're holding the bat wrong."

He tried to turn the boy around. But each time, the boy kept trying to hit left-handed. The next boy did the same. And the next. The coach vainly kept turning them around, explaining that they were doing it wrong, but he made no progress, and then he figured it out. They were simply doing what any good Kansas City child would do. They were simply trying to hit like George Brett.

AP/Wide World Photos

Brett kisses home plate after playing his final game in Kansas City in 1993.

THE KANSAS CITY STAR.

"I was there for the game at Royals Stadium when George Brett hit the double to go over .400. And I remember that after he got his big hit, he stood on second base and raised his arms. And at that moment, it was like he was the king of the world. There was nothing George Brett couldn't do. We all believed that. All of us."
—Bob Kealing

Staff Photo, The Kansas City Star

Brett at spring training in Florida.

George Brett connected with fans in a way that seems unlikely forevermore. Baseball has changed. Sure, there's more money in the game now, more hype, more teams, more Hollywood—heck, Disney, Turner and Fox all own teams—but no, it's something else. Brett played when baseball players were more solid somehow. You could count on them. They showed up every day, played hurt, got dirty, did not demand to be traded all the time. They lived in town; you would see them at the bar after the game or in the supermarket during the off-season. It was a different time. Baseball cards were a dime a pack, nobody sold autographs, the game of the week was Saturday afternoons, the whole thing just seemed more innocent. On the field, George Brett was your friend.

"Sure, I had a different relationship with the fans than the guys today," Brett says. "But you have to remember, I wasn't making $10 million either. I was making good money for the time, but nothing like that. I was scraping along just like everybody else. People related to that."

"My memory goes back to September 1976. It was in Texas, and I was wearing all my Royals garb. I was watching George Brett warming up. I called down to him and asked him to throw me a ball. He nodded. A few minutes later, a friend pointed down the field, and I heard George yell. He threw the ball. I saw it float at me in slow motion.

"It was way over my head. The ball landed five or seven rows behind me. I rushed to get it, but a concession girl picked it up first. I said, 'George Brett threw me that ball.' She handed it to another fan.

"I was depressed. I looked down on the field again. And I heard George Brett say, 'Nice catch.'"
—J.T. Beckman

GEORGE BRETT
Essay by Joe Posnanski

Brett with his wife, Leslie, and Jim Woodard at a benefit for the ALS foundation.

Brett acknowledges the crowd during ceremonies retiring his Royals jersey.

Brett reads BABAR SAVES THE DAY with Ricky King during a program promoting children's literacy.

More people ask him about the pine-tar home run than anything else. It's a funny thing that Brett's noble career would be reduced to a few manic seconds where he sped from the dugout like a madman and rushed an umpire who was 50 pounds heavier than him, but then, that was what Kansas City loved about George Brett. He was a fighter.

"You know, before it even happened, I knew I would go crazy," Brett said. He hit the home run off Goose Gossage, and there was always something special when those two faced off anyway. Gossage threw what, next to Nolan Ryan, was probably the fastest fastball in the major leagues, always near 100 mph, and, unlike Ryan, he threw it with a scowl.

Nobody hit fastballs like George Brett.

So every time those two faced off, it was epic, a heavyweight fight, and this time Gossage threw a high fastball, and Brett mashed it, a two-run homer that gave the Royals the lead, and that was when Billy Martin, manager of the Yankees, decided to have the bat inspected.

There's an obscure baseball rule that prevents batters from having any pine tar 18 inches above the handle of the bat. Martin called for the rule. Umpire Tim McClelland measured and saw that there was too much pine tar. He took away Brett's home run. Brett went absolutely bananas.

Later, the home run was given back to him, but somehow that moment of Brett charging the 6-foot-6, 250-pound McClelland, arms waving, swear words flying, somehow that moment has endured. People could relate to the man, fighting against ambiguous rules, charging authority, what could be more American than that? He was Dirty Harry and George Washington and Harry Truman.

Then again, maybe it was just fun to watch a man completely lose his mind.

"I guess it's good that it happened," Brett says. "Otherwise, people would only remember me for hemorrhoids."

"It was a Saturday game against the Red Sox. The score was something like 2-2, and Luis Tiant was pitching for Boston. It was the bottom of the 10th, and as I remember, Brett hit Tiant's first pitch into the right-field general-admission seats. The crowd roared, but what I remember is that even Luis Tiant smiled. It's that smile I remember. Even in that loss, he was happy for George. That's a Hall of Famer for you."
—Chris O'Shea

Keith Myers, The Kansas City Star

Kansas City and the Royals celebrate with a parade following the 1985 World Series.

George Brett dominated every game he played. That was his gift. There are few players like that. Sometimes, people will go to a game, buy a program, and only years later, when they look at it, will they realize that they saw Rod Carew play or Robin Yount, only then will they remember that they watched Gaylord Perry pitch or Steve Carlton. Basketball is an individual sport, nobody can forget seeing Michael Jordan or Magic Johnson or Larry Bird. But baseball is a happening, an experience, full of sights, sounds, mustard, sunshine, beer, organs, fountains, grass, sticky floors, baseballs flying into the stands. One player does not overwhelm the rest.

George Brett did. Every moment, you were aware how many more batters until Brett came up again. While he stood at third base, every parent pointed him out to their children. Every time he came to the plate, it was an event, a party, that was why people had come to the ballpark. No game was over if George Brett had another at-bat.

"He had that charisma that made him different," says his old teammate, Frank White. "Obviously, George was a great player, but he also had that presence about him. Opponents feared him. We counted on him. You knew he was going to do something every day to help the ballclub win. We would take the field, and we were cocky back then, and I think we were thinking 'Hey, we have George Brett, and you don't.'"

"I keep thinking how great it was watching George Brett when I was a kid. He seemed so much larger than life. My father told me to watch his every move. I used to watch him closely. Then, when I got home, I tried to do everything just like he did. I tried to swing the bat like him. I tried to throw like him. I tried to field ground balls like him.

"I watch baseball these days, and I feel sorry for my son. He will never have George Brett. I watch these players, and I wonder: Who will my son pretend to be when he gets home?"
—Jeremy Smith

Keith Myers, The Kansas City Star

George Brett hammers a pitch during spring training.

George Brett often said he wanted his last at-bat to be a ground ball to second base. That way he could run like mad and try to beat it out. That, he figured, would be a fitting wrap to his career, a nice summation of the way he played baseball.

"To me, the greatest thing in the world to be was a ballplayer," Brett says. "I never wanted to be anything else. I never wanted to be a star. I never wanted to be a millionaire. I just wanted to be a ballplayer."

"Sixteen years after my husband and I went on our first date to a Royals game in Kansas City, we were at Arlington Stadium to watch one of George Brett's last games.

"We remembered that long-ago spring day of 1977, I had agreed to go out with a young man I met at work. I remember how he rhapsodized about No. 5, the Royals' third baseman. He pointed out the intricacies of Brett's batting stance, the fluidity of his swing, the fact that he didn't wear batting gloves so he could get a better feel of the bat.

"As we sat in the bleachers that day, 16 years later, my husband and I reflected on Brett's career—and our life together."
—Vicki Marsh-Kabat

David Pulliam, The Kansas City Star

Brett signs autographs at the 1997 dedication
of the George Brett Bridge in Kansas City.

In the days before the Hall of Fame vote, George Brett stirred and bounced around and basically went bananas. Everybody assured him he was in. Reporters called to ask what it felt like to be so close. Indeed, deep down, he must have understood that, surely, they would vote him in because, well, how could they deny him? He had been as good a player as any of his generation. He had chased .400 and beaten the Yankees, he flourished under the World Series lights, ran out every ground ball, banged more doubles than anyone of his time, he even won a Gold Glove for defensive excellence one season, 1985, perhaps his proudest achievement.

He had done everything, and he had done all of it gracefully.

He was a player for all time.

Still, he could not sleep as the Hall of Fame vote approached.

"Yeah, everybody was saying that I was in," he would say. "But I couldn't help but think that they were just telling me that, you know? Hey, they're my friends; of course they're going to say that. No, until I got the phone call, I just didn't believe it."

He got the phone call, and it turned out he received 98.19 percent of the votes, the fourth-highest total of all time, and at the news conference he broke down, but not

before saying, "This is the dream."

Only then could he explain why the Hall of Fame meant so much to him. He had played baseball all his life, and he loved it like nobody of his time. He loved the game, and he loved the clubhouse, and he loved practical jokes, and he loved the bars afterward, and he loved the cheers. He loved the poker games, and he loved playing golf with teammates for a few bucks, and he loved coming to the plate with runners on second and third and the game on the line.

Yes, he loved it, and he got rich off it, and he heard the loudest cheers all over America, and he felt the warmest embrace of Kansas City, and he lived a good life. But, still, he wanted that Hall of Fame. He wanted it so much.

And when they voted him in, he felt intoxicated.

His dream had come true.

They had called him a ballplayer.

Lauren Chapin, The Kansas City Star

Brett joins Connie Johnson (left), Alfred "Slick" Surratt, and James "Lefty" LaMarque (right) at the opening of the Negro Leagues Baseball Museum in Kansas City.

THE KANSAS CITY STAR.

GEORGE BRETT
Essay by Joe Posnanski

AFTERMATH: Nobody's quite sure what George Brett does for the Kansas City Royals these days, least of all Brett himself. He's listed as a vice president/baseball operations, but those are corporate words, and what the heck do those words mean anyway? He shows up for games. He hangs out at the ballpark occasionally. He has an office at Kauffman Stadium.

No, the only time he's sure of himself is during spring training. Brett loves spring training. He wasn't crazy about it as a player—Brett was a notoriously slow starter—but he loves being around the kids, loves teaching them card tricks or taking some of their money at the poker table. Their enthusiasm stokes him. If they ask, he teaches them a bit about hitting, too.

One day, in spring 1999, he talked Royals manager Tony Muser into a money-ball scheme. Brett marked one of the baseballs, and Muser put up 100 bucks for the player who brought in the marked baseball.

So, after practice, Brett told everybody about the money ball. And they all ran out to the outfield to gather the thousand baseballs, hoping to find the money ball. In the middle of it all, there was Brett, knocking down players, scooping up baseballs, searching desperately for the marked baseball.

"That son of a gun," Muser said. "No wonder he came up with this scheme. He wants my hundred bucks. The man's going to the Hall of Fame, and he wants my hundred bucks."

Muser just shook his head as Brett kept running around the outfield in his Royals uniform, bumping into the kids, diving in the grass, screaming like a school kid, laughing his head off, reaching for stray baseballs.

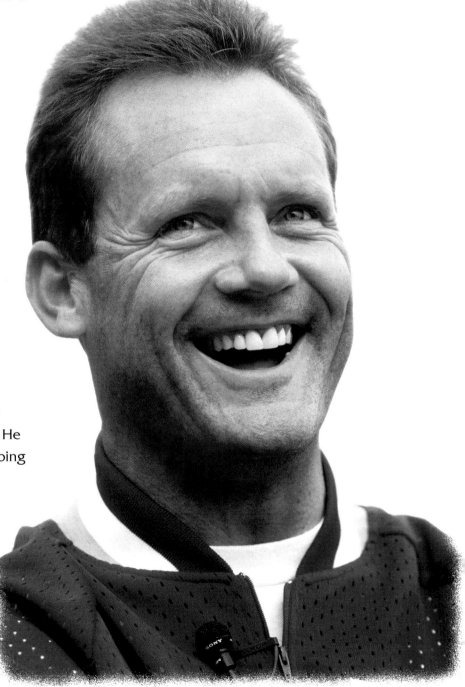

Staff Photo, The Kansas City Star

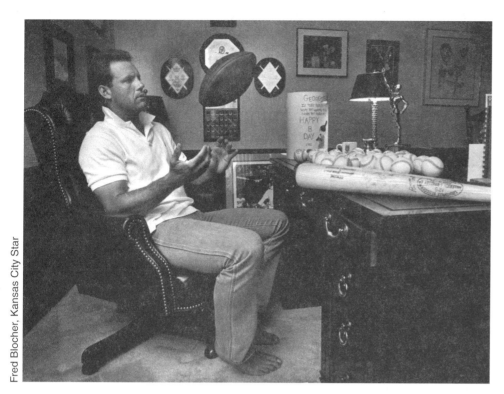

Sports memorabilia surround George Brett in his home, including a signed Joe Namath football and a trash can full of baseballs.

He flicked casually past the ball that bore the impression of hit No. 200 in his first 200-hit season of 1976. Another ball, this one from September 15, 1979, against Seattle, marked his 100th RBI that year.

"I don't remember who was pitching," Brett said. "But that was the first time I drove in 100 runs.

"I guess the ones by the presidents are special too. I've never met Nixon. I met Reagan and met Ford."

But on the wall behind his desk it is a hand-written letter from Richard Nixon that Brett treasures.

"The letter says: 'One who roots for the home team. I am a Yankee fan and a longtime George Brett fan. I thought you got a lousy deal (the original pine-tar ruling voided Brett's home run). I'll wager they change the rule in the future. In the meantime keep slugging. With warmest regards, Richard Nixon.'

"I thought that was really nice. Whenever he writes a book, he sends me an autographed copy. The Richard Nixon ball I got in Anaheim after he was through being president. One night I heard he was at the game and I sent a ball up with somebody and told them I would appreciate it if they could get him to sign it for me. Sure enough, after the game it was there in my locker. From that came the letter and the books. He is an interesting man."

The balls from El Segundo, Calif., and his high school years also mean something special. The one from O'Bradovich came when a high school friend won a slow-pitch batting title.

Since then Brett has turned on a few crowds of his own, and an aspiring young baseball player could do worse than walk onto the field alongside Brett and hear the fans cheer.

Brett would understand.

He still remembers his heroes.

He just keeps his memories in the trash can.

Champion Talker

August 4, 1986

George Brett noticed on a plane that his seatmate had on a "Royals World Champion" hat. "I thought, 'Oh, no, I've got some guy who will bust my chops the entire flight, wanting to know why the Royals aren't winning,'" *Sports Illustrated* quoted Mr. Brett as saying. It turned out that the man was actor Patrick Duffy of "Dallas." "I told him 'Dallas' is my favorite show and I proceeded to bust his chops about it all the way to Houston."

july 12, 1986

by The Kansas City Star

Injury to Keep Brett Out of All-Star Game

Royals third baseman George Brett, who was elected to his 11th consecutive All-Star Game this week, has been replaced on the American League roster by Cleveland's Brook Jacoby because of a shoulder injury, the league announced Friday.

Boston's Wade Boggs, who was second in the voting behind Brett, probably will be chosen to replace Brett in the starting lineup, AL Vice President Bob Fishel said. Brett, however, plans to be in uniform but won't play in the game, which is scheduled for Tuesday in Houston.

Brett has been suffering from strained shoulder ligaments and a strained rotator-cuff tendon in his right shoulder since a July 1 game in Seattle.

1986 American League All-Star Starting Lineup

Position	Player	Team	Avg.	HR	RBI
Catcher	Lance Parrish	Detroit	.262	21	59
First	Wally Joyner	California	.303	20	67
Second	Lou Whitaker	Detroit	.271	11	36
Third	**George Brett**	**Kansas City**	**.290**	**8**	**40**
Shortstop	Cal Ripken	Baltimore	.294	12	46
Outfield	Kirby Puckett	Minnesota	.342	16	49
Outfield	Rickey Henderson	New York	.279	15	48
Outfield	Dave Winfield	New York	.233	13	55

1986

by Bob Nightengale

Operation on Brett's Shoulder Is Called a Success

A torn cartilage and a small piece of the clavicle were removed from the right shoulder of Royals third baseman George Brett this morning in a 45-minute operation in Los Angeles, the Royals said today.

The Royals also said that Brett is expected to be ready for the opening of spring training.

"The cartilage," Royals trainer Mickey Cobb said, "was the reason for all his problems. There shouldn't be any more problems now."

The operation was performed by Dr. Frank Jobe at Centinela Medical Center in Los Angeles, who told the Royals the operation was a success. Cobb said Jobe told him in a phone conversation that Brett's shoulder should be fit after two months of rehabilitation. Thus, Brett should not miss any of spring training. The Royals' first exhibition game is scheduled March 6.

Brett missed 38 games last season because of the aching right shoulder and was unable to lift his right arm above his head after more than a month of rest after the season.

Brett will remain hospitalized for two days, Cobb said, and his shoulder will be in a sling for two to three weeks before the start of rehabilitation.

George's Job Satisfaction

December 15, 1986

The December issue of Esquire, dedicated to work, asked various folks about their professions. Kansas City Royals third baseman George Brett was asked whether he believed his job "was worth the time."

"Playing baseball beats working for a living," he replied. "It beats being a bartender. But it's tough to have people everywhere you go yelling at you about hemorrhoids and pine tar. You just get tired of it after a while. Other than that, though, it's pretty nice."

1986

Jim McTaggart, Kansas City Star

He was always the guy—he was the clutch guy. Not only with the manager, coaches and his teammates, but the fans knew more often than not in a clutch situation he'd come through because he was so mentally tough and accepted being that guy.

—Denny Matthews,
Royals radio announcer

A Change of Base

By May of 1987, George Brett was on his third injury of the season. A partial tear of the medial collateral ligament in his right knee was the 26th injury of his career. Frustrated about his injury-prone career, Brett also began to feel the resentment of his teammates and fans weighing down on him.

He was eager to get back in the swing of things when he returned to the lineup in mid-June. Brett was selected to the All-Star team at third base, but because of a shoulder injury he had to give up his spot to teammate Kevin Seitzer. Seitzer, a rookie, would not only replace Brett on the All-Star roster, but he would assume Brett's third-base duties for the duration of Brett's injury and beyond. George Brett was now a first baseman.

Disappointed with his season and determined to disprove critics of his abilities, Brett planned to use the off-season to work himself back to top form. "I want to prove them wrong; I want to prove them all wrong," Brett said.

april 27, 1987

by Bob Nightengale

Brett Says He's Feeling Resentment from Teammates

DETROIT—The words were haunting. This is an 11-year All-Star. He's a man who's more readily identified with the Royals' organization than anyone in franchise history.

Yet, after suffering a cartilage separation in his right rib cage April 19—the 14th injury of his career, which will sideline him for a minimum of eight games—Brett senses resentment by his teammates.

"I don't think a lot of people understand how much I love this game, how I love to perform in front of people," Brett said. "Some days, you stink the joint up. But I'll tell you what, I'd rather go 0 for four than sitting here like I am now and watching 'My Three Sons.'"

Jack Brett, George's father, said: "George told me he gets the feeling that they're looking at him funny. He feels like they think he should play. He gets those looks and takes those as looks of reprimand."

Compounding Brett's anguish, once again, is his value to the team. When Brett is injured, the entire complexion of the Royals' lineup changes. And more often than not, the ultimate result is defeat.

The Royals were shut out four of the first five games during Brett's absence and own a 3-5 record since Brett was injured.

The Royals, overall, are 110-126 (46.6 percent) in games that Brett has missed during the 14 injuries.

"He's very aware of that," Jack Brett said. "When I talked to him last week, he kept talking about the shutouts. He knows the guys need him."

George Brett's "Lifetime Contract"

NAME: George Brett
BASE SALARY: $1.5 million
EXPIRATION: 1991, club options 1992-1993
INCENTIVES: $100,000 for MVP, $50,000 each for World Series MVP/American League playoffs MVP; $50,000 All-Star team; $100,000 Gold Glove; $60,000 for 550 plate appearances; $100,000 for 625 plate appearances.
SIGNING BONUS: None.
EXTRAS: Seven-year personal-services contract for $75,000 minimum as vice president upon retirement; $5 million loan with 10 percent interest; 10 percent interest in Country Squire Ltd., a housing development in Memphis, Tenn., with minimum guaranteed cash flow of $1 million by December 1991; 10 percent partnership may be sold in 1991 for $2 million, $2.25 million in 1992 or $2.5 million in 1993. Single room on road trips.

1987

may 21, 1987

by Bob Nightengale

Injuries Jeopardize Brett's Bid for Hall

F or the 26th time in his career and third time this season, Brett is injured. This time, the injury is a partial tear in the medial collateral ligament of his right knee. But this one is no easier to cope with than his first injury in 1977 when he missed 13 games because of a sore right elbow.

Brett now has missed 282 games in his career solely because of injuries. Already this

season, he has missed two games because of a hamstring pull, 19 games because of a pulled rib cage muscle and five games and counting because of his knee injury.

By the time Brett returns from this injury, which is expected to be at least three more weeks, he'll be close to missing two full major-league seasons because of injuries.

14-Year Comparisons

Brett vs. Some of the Best Since 1945

Player	YR	G	AG	AB	R	H	2B	3B	HR	RBI	AVG
George Brett	14	1741	124	6675	1072	2095	428	112	209	1050	.314
Hank Aaron	14	2119	151	8283	1519	2618	451	84	481	1541	.316
Rod Carew	14	1889	134	7184	1075	2394	354	100	80	836	.333
Roberto Clemente	14	1953	140	7635	1114	2384	350	129	184	1008	.312
Joe DiMaggio	13	1736	136	6821	1390	2214	389	131	361	1537	.325
Reggie Jackson	14	1924	137	6863	1145	1874	345	41	410	1231	.273
Al Kaline	14	1862	133	6857	1115	2087	344	62	279	1117	.304
Mickey Mantle	14	1883	135	6533	1473	2016	289	69	454	1298	.309
Eddie Mathews	14	2086	149	7597	1380	2088	317	66	477	1335	.275
Willie Mays	14	2005	143	7594	1497	2381	375	118	505	1402	.314
Stan Musial	14	1988	142	7590	1493	2597	539	156	325	1361	.342
Dave Parker	14	1779	127	6727	978	2024	397	69	247	1093	.301
Frank Robinson	14	2064	147	7542	1428	2283	421	65	450	1377	.303
Pete Rose	14	2184	156	8886	1459	2762	483	101	134	838	.310
Mike Schmidt	14	1947	139	6740	1252	1794	323	56	458	1273	.266
Billy Williams	14	1940	139	7499	1179	2231	358	85	356	1199	.298
Ted Williams	14	1679	120	5893	1462	2051	416	66	394	1470	.348
Carl Yastrzemski	14	2117	151	7759	1240	2267	436	47	303	1181	.292

1987

june 13, 1987

by Jonathan Rand

Return Is a Test for Brett

Bret Saberhagen, the Royals' starting pitcher Friday night, must have had a premonition where his support would be coming from.

Saberhagen, on the bench during batting practice, asked trainer Mickey Cobb: "Is George playing tonight?"

George Brett, whose fourth-inning double drove in the only run Saberhagen needed in a 1-0 victory over the California Angels, had been cleared to make his return after a four-week absence.

It's been a long time between at-bats."

Manager Billy Gardner said Brett would remain the DH for a few games before returning to third base. Brett has missed 45 games because of thigh, rib-cage and knee injuries.

"It was frustrating even when we were winning because when you're winning, everybody's having a lot of fun," Brett said. "I wasn't having any fun.

"I would've taken an 0 for 5 with a couple of errors. That would've been more fun than sitting around, watching them play.

> **At least you're out there working up a sweat and feeling like part of the team. I haven't felt like a part of the team all year long.**
>
> **—George Brett**

"I got a lot of 'welcome backs,' and that always makes you feel good," Brett said, referring to the responses of fans and teammates.

"Little did I know at the time that would be the only run of the game. I feel good now.

"At least you're out there working up a sweat and feeling like part of the team. I haven't felt like a part of the team all year long."

His feeling was a whole lot different Friday night.

1987

Saberhagen, Brett Are AL All-Stars

TORONTO—While Bret Saberhagen realized one of his childhood dreams by being selected Thursday to pitch in the All-Star Game, teammate George Brett was somewhat embarrassed by the honor and did not believe it was fair that he was invited.

Saberhagen and Brett were the only Royals selected to play in the All-Star Game. Saberhagen will be making his first All-Star appearance, and Brett was selected for the 12th consecutive year.

For Brett, who has been voted as the staring third basemen in 11 straight All-Star Games before losing out to Wade Boggs of the Boston Red Sox this season, his nomination was rather surprising.

Brett has missed 45 games this season because of injuries. And although he entered Thursday's game with a .321 batting average, he still has only seven homers and 30 RBIs.

Jamie Quirk, Brett's closest friend on the team, said: "I think he's embarrassed. It's his pride. I'm sure he'd like to have 15 homers and 50 RBIs and probably is embarrassed with the numbers he's got."

Boy, Was That Last Caller Way off Base!

Tony Rizzo
May 25, 1987

A fan concerned about George Brett's latest injury may have feared that the Royals third baseman's condition was more serious than he thought.

The man tried to call the Royals office last week but instead dialed the number for the Lawrence A. Jones funeral home in Kansas City.

He asked for public relations and was connected with Lindsay Jones, who handles P.R. for the funeral home.

"I wanted to check on the seriousness of George Brett's condition," the man told Jones.

"This is the Lawrence A. Jones funeral home," Jones told him. "I don't think the status of his injuries have become that severe."

Jones said he and the man both got a big laugh out of the incident.

1987

by Jack Etkin

Hobbled Again, Brett Decides to Surrender All-Star Spot

Rookie Seitzer Added to AL Team

TORONTO—George Brett, whose ailing right shoulder prevented him from playing first base Saturday, has been replaced on the American League All-Star team by teammate Kevin Seitzer.

The decision was announced Saturday morning by Royals Manager Billy Gardner, who had talked to American League President Bobby Brown.

"In a way, I would have loved to be at the game," said Brett, who was selected Thursday as the backup third baseman to starter Wade Boggs of Boston, "but I didn't want to go there and not help the team win."

Instead Brett will spend his All-Star break in Los Angeles, where he has an 11:30 a.m. (central time) appointment Monday with orthopedic specialist Dr. Frank Jobe. Jobe and Dr. Lewis Yocum removed a folded piece of cartilage and a small piece of the clavicle from Brett's right shoulder last November. Brett missed 42 games last year after injuring the shoulder July 1 diving for a ground ball.

"It's the same shoulder but a different area," Brett said. "I think it's muscular. Before it was bone."

Brett said that while he cannot throw, his shoulder does not prevent him from swinging a bat.

Brett was pleased that Seitzer was chosen to replace him on the AL team, "He deserves to be there," Brett said. "He's done a tremendous job offensively and defensively. It's a good experience for a young kid like that, not that it wouldn't be a good experience for an old guy, too."

Veteran Brett Set to Accept Third-Base Job Is Seitzer's

by Bob Nightengale
July 16, 1987

For 13 straight seasons in the Royals' glory years, third base has been manned by only one person. Oh sure, George Brett had injuries and missed more than his share of games, but there was no doubt Brett was the third baseman.

Yet, when the Royals begin the second half of their season at 7:35 tonight against the Baltimore Orioles at Royals Stadium, No. 5 will no longer be found at third.

Brett is now a first baseman and may never return to the other side of the infield.

Kevin Seitzer, a 25-year-old rookie, represents the Royals' new regime and possibly could remain at third for the rest of his career.

The greatest thing he taught me was on my first day in the big leagues—it was the hustle. He hit two one-hoppers to the pitcher and ran as hard as he could to first base. He set a great example for me to model my career. His hustle and desire—those were the little things that stood out for me.

—Kevin Seitzer, Brett's successor at third base

by Bob Nightengale

Brett Begins Working on Return to Stardom

RANCHO MIRAGE, Calif.—Tucked away between the mountains and surrounded by palm trees and golf courses, Rancho Mirage is only a 2 $\frac{1}{2}$ hour drive from Los Angeles, but it might as well be a different planet.

The homes in this community *start* at $200,000, and you can bet the neighbors—which include Frank Sinatra, Bob Hope, Gerald Ford and Dinah Shore—live in fancier digs. Mercedes, Porches, Ferrais, Jaguars and Rolls-Royces provide the chic decor for every garage.

Well, maybe not every *one*.

Inside the garage of the Spanish villa on Sunningdale Street, the one overlooking the 15th fairway, is the makings of a gymnasium.

There is a punching bag and a heavy bag on one side of the garage. On the other, there is a hitting tee, a net, a box of baseballs and a carton of bats. And against the wall there is a 10-speed bike, complete with new tires and gears.

"I'll be spending my winter a little differently from other folks around here," said George Brett, who makes his living playing baseball for the Royals and wants to keep it that way.

With the prompting of a telephone call two weeks ago Sunday from Royals co-owner Avron Fogelman, Brett began a rigorous conditioning program that he hopes will return him to baseball's elite.

"A lot of people out there feel my career is on a downhill slide," Brett said. "They think I'm getting old, that I'm in the twilight of my career. And there are some that think I'm lying down because I have a big contract.

"I want to prove them wrong; I want to prove them all wrong."

Fogelman suggested strongly that Brett proceed immediately with his conditioning program without wasting any further time.

"I had a conversation with him just like I did in '84," Fogelman said. "I talked about what were his best interests, and as far as the Royals' interest. I just told him how important it is that he comes to spring training in good condition, and I think George needed someone to tell him that.

"George was very, very responsive. I think he appreciated the concern. He told me that he would give a total commitment to his rededication to the training program that he had three years ago."

Brett believes the season that followed that training program, 1985, was the finest of his career: .335 average, 30 homers, 112 RBIs, a Gold Glove and a World Series Championship.

"I think I proved to myself in '84 the benefits of working out," Brett said. "I want to benefit again. I proved it before, and I want to prove it again.

"I think there are a lot of George Brett fans in Kansas City, but there are a lot of people out there who aren't George Brett fans. If I haven't made an impression on those people, or gained their respect for what I've accomplished in my career, I never will. I don't care about those people.

"The people I'm doing this for are the ones who have stood behind me throughout the years. I'm doing this for my family. I'm doing this for the Royals' organization. I'm doing this for my friends.

"Most of all, I'm doing this for myself."

Brett, for the first time in his illustrious career, has suffered what for him are considered two successive mediocre seasons. Hampered by injuries, he hit .290 each of the last two seasons, averaging 19 homers and 76 RBIs.

It was the first time Brett batted below .300 in consecutive seasons since 1974.

For now, the situation has him feeling uncomfortable and embarrassed.

"This is bothering him; it's upsetting him quite a bit," said Ken Brett, George's older brother. "Before, you mention the name, 'George Brett,' and you ask, 'Is he the top player in the game?'

AP/Wide World Photos

After two mediocre seasons, George Brett hopes to improve his numbers by working out in the off-season.

"But now, they haven't mentioned his name in that light in two years. Sure, he's still a recognizable and big name, but he doesn't have numbers.

"And that kills him."

"I know I'm getting old," said Brett, 34. "I can accept that. And I know the Astro Turf can take it out of you. But what I can't accept is what I've done the last two years. They've been extremely tough years to live with.

"And last year, well, that's as low as I've ever been in my career."

Bob Nightengale
November 18, 1987

To expedite his progress at first base, Brett brought home a couple of first baseman's mitts. You can imagine golfers' surprise when they see Brett's good friend, pro golfer Fred Couples, firing away with his 8-iron on the driving range and Brett scrambling to catch the golf balls with his glove.

"It gets a little tougher when Freddy brings out his driver," Brett said.

This may be the start of something new in the way of first basemen's training if Brett has the type of year he envisions.

1987

I'm 35 and at that point where I've got to put out or ship out, basically.

—George Brett

1988

Proving Himself

The Royals were looking to Brett to lead them to the postseason in 1988. After a brief scare in which he injured a tendon in his hand, Brett rolled into the season. He crushed a home run out of Tiger Stadium, making him only the 15th batter to clear the roof.

Brett was selected to the All-Star team for the 13th time of his career, this time at first base. For the first time in three years, he was in playing form for the game.

Determined to re-establish himself as one of the best hitters in baseball, Brett's numbers went on a roller-coaster ride. In July, he was batting .394, but he took a dive in early August, hitting .228 throughout most of the month. By the end of the season, however, Brett finished with a satisfying .306 average, having played in 157 games—the most he had played in during 13 seasons.

by Bob Nightengale

Royals Look to Ride Brett to West Title

HAINES CITY, Fla.—The Royals' first full-squad workout just ended Wednesday afternoon when first baseman George Brett busily contemplated how he would spend the rest of the afternoon.

It was too late to sneak in a round of golf. Too nice of a day to sit in the clubhouse and play cards. So ...

Can you imagine the look on Royals General Manager John Schuerholz's face if he glanced out of his office window and saw Brett riding the roller coaster at the Boardwalk and Baseball amusement park?

It hardly is the type of activity Schuerholz wants to see from the man who is expected to determine the Royals' fate in the 1988 season.

"He's so dynamic, so strong, so capable," Schuerholz said, "that we have to rely on him. You've got to have a few good players to have a shot at the World Series, but you also have to have that great player. He's that player.

"And it bothers me because I don't think the world really understands and appreciates how good he is. If you could pick any player to start a franchise, how could you not pick George Brett?"

If healthy, the numbers will fall in line. Never in his 14-year career has he failed to hit below .300 when playing in at least 128 games.

Staff photo, Kansas City Star

Golf is a favorite off-season activity for George Brett. The George Brett Celebrity Golf Tournament raises money for ALS.

And if healthy, Brett hopes the respect that once accompanied his name will return.

"I want back.

"And I will be back."

march 31, 1988

by Bob Nightengale

Brett Wants to Have Great Year for Dad

HAINES CITY, Fla.—Three weeks ago George Brett sat on his bed with a phone to his ear, trying to keep from crying, hoping his voice would stop quivering.

Ken Brett, George's older brother, was informing him that their father, Jack, had clogged arteries and was about to undergo open-heart surgery.

Brett, after regaining his composure on that March 10 afternoon, telephoned his father and found him in a mood to reveal his innermost feeling toward his youngest son.

The game of baseball suddenly seemed trivial to Brett, the Royals' first baseman. And yet, after talking to his father, the game perhaps became more important to Brett than ever before.

Never having attended a World Series game or any of Brett's 43 postseason games, Jack Brett rarely has acknowledged his son's baseball feats. With Brett entering his 15th major league season, Jack Brett thought he better tell him his dreams now.

"There's only one thing I want to do before I do die," Jack Brett told his son, "and that's to go to Cooperstown.

"I want to go back to see you inducted into the Hall of Fame. But you haven't made it yet. You still have a lot of things you have to accomplish in your career. Let's start now."

Brett, after detailing the emotional conversation and saying that his father is recovering nicely from his March 11 operation, said, "I guess I've known all along he'd like me to make it. Even when I was in Little League, he wanted all his sons to make it. And right now, I'm the only one who has a chance to make it.

"But I think for the first time in my life it made me realize the importance of what I do, not only to myself, but to other people. How happy it makes him when I have good games. How happy it makes my three brothers. How happy it makes my friends in Kansas City or Los Angeles.

"That's a lot of inspiration to do better than you think you're capable of doing. It gives you that extra incentive.

"But I've got to go out and perform at that level in which I performed before, and I haven't done that the last few years."

"But it's not something where you go out and say, 'I want to have a good year so I could make the Hall of Fame,'" Brett said. "That's not why you go out and try to have a good year. You want to go out and have a good year so you can help your ballclub win.

"Then when you're through playing, and if you're inducted in the Hall of Fame, that's the greatest honor you could ever ask for. Spend 20 years doing a job, and then all of a sudden, be considered one of the best.

"That'd be a tremendous honor.

"It's something I want to do very badly for my father."

by Bob Nightengale

Brett Not Hurt Badly, Expected to Start Opener

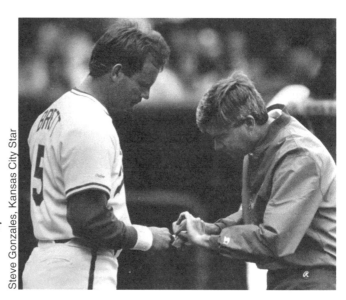

Steve Gonzales, Kansas City Star

HAINES City, Fla.—George Brett caused a panic throughout the Royals' camp Friday when his ailing finger prevented him from taking batting practice, but it proved to be nothing more than a scare.

Brett was diagnosed in Kansas City as having a bruised ligament on the middle finger of his right hand and will be able to play Monday in the Royals' season opener against the Toronto Blue Jays.

"I'm relieved, obviously," Royals Manager John Wathan said. "I think he'll be able to play Monday. You've got to know George, how bad he wants to play on opening day."

Assistant trainer Paul McGannon adds tape to the finger of George Brett, who bruised a ligament in his right hand.

1988

Publisher Gets Apology for Incident with Brett

April 14, 1988

The Royals have reprimanded George Brett, and General Manager John Schuerholz has apologized to Tom Leathers for the spring-training incident in which Brett smashed Leathers' camera.

Schuerholz said in a letter to Leathers: "George was reprimanded immediately by me and our field manager, John Wathan …"

The letter continued: "We are very sorry this unfortunate incident took place, and on behalf of the Royals' organization we extend our sincerest apologies."

Leathers, the publisher of The Squire and The Squire's Other Paper, said Wednesday that he considered the matter closed.

april 18, 1988

by Bob Nightengale

Brett Blasts Way into a Most Elite Group

DETROIT—George Brett hit the ball with all his might in the fourth inning Sunday, but instead of running, he stood and watched the ball soar above the upper-deck seats … above the roof, until it disappeared.

"I just lost it after that," Brett said.

The ball actually skipped off the Tiger Stadium roof, bounced once on Trumbull Avenue and landed in the Brooks Lumberyard across the street.

It was just the 22nd home run hit out of Tiger Stadium since it was remodeled in 1938 and the first home run to clear the roof since September 10, 1986, when former Tiger Kirk Gibson hit one off Chris Bosio of Milwaukee. It was the first home run hit out of Tiger Stadium by a visiting player since Reggie Jackson did it on May 12, 1984.

"It's the furthest I've ever hit a ball in my life," said Brett, whose homer, hit on a 1-2 fastball off Jeff Robinson, was estimated by Detroit officials at about 450 feet. "I've put a lot into the upper deck at Yankee Stadium, and I hit one in the upper deck in Seattle off Floyd Bannister, but nothing like this.

"It's a great feeling to hit a ball that hard, that high, that far. It's a great, great thrill. It's one I'll never forget."

Brett, so excited by the majestic blast, said he almost forgot to run. He stood at the plate watching the ball's flight longer than he can ever remember before beginning his home-run trot.

"Very seldom do I watch my home runs," Brett said, "and I didn't want to show anyone up. But that one, I just wanted to sit back and enjoy it."

Clearing the Roof

George Brett became the 15th batter to hit a home run over the roof and out of Tiger Stadium since the stadium was rebuilt along its present lines in 1938. There have been 22 home runs hit over the roof and out of Tiger Stadium since 1938.

Batter, Team	Date
George Brett, Kansas City	**April 17, 1988**
Kirk Gibson, Detroit	Sept. 10, 1986
Lou Whitaker, Detroit	May 13, 1985
Ruppert Jones, Detroit	June 24, 1984
Reggie Jackson, California	May 12, 1984
Cecil Cooper, Milwaukee	Oct. 2, 1983
Kirk Gibson, Detroit	June 14, 1983
Jason Thompson, Detroit	Sept. 17, 1977
Jason Thompson, Detroit	Aug. 18, 1977
Jim Northrup, Detroit	Aug. 28, 1969
Boog Powell, Baltimore	July 6, 1969
Frank Howard, Washington	May 18, 1968
Don Mincher, Minnesota	Aug. 23, 1967
Harmon Killebrew, Minnesota	Aug. 3, 1962
Norm Cash, Detroit	July 29, 1962
Norm Cash, Detroit	July 27, 1962
Norm Cash, Detroit	May 11, 1962
Norm Cash, Detroit	June 11, 1961
Mickey Mantle, New York	Sept. 10, 1960
Mickey Mantle, New York	Sept. 17, 1958
Mickey Mantle, New York	June 18, 1956
Ted Williams, Boston	May 4, 1939

1988

by Jonathan Rand

All-Star Selection Is Still Special for Brett

1988

His selection to the American League All-Star team brings George Brett one more pleasant reminder that he is making good on his determination to put his name back on the marquee of major-league baseball.

"I'm 35 and at that point where I've got to put out or ship out, basically," Brett said.

Until this season, Brett was an almost automatic All-Star choice. He was voted to start at third base 11 straight years, most recently in 1986, although he was hitting below .300 and runner-up Wade Boggs was leading the league.

Brett sat out that game because of a shoulder injury, as he did last year's game after being added to the team despite missing 45 games.

Brett is among those charismatic players All-Star fans want to see as long as they still can button their uniforms. He will go in Tuesday through the front door.

After three hits and two runs batted in Thursday, he is hitting .338, with 13 home runs and 61 RBIs.

If ever there was a season in which Brett's streak of All-Star berths seemed endangered, this was it. For the first time, he had to make the squad at first base, a position loaded with marquee names. Brett and the Yankees' Don Mattingly were added to the squad, behind the Athletics' Mark McGwire.

"It means a lot because I didn't think I had a prayer to make it," Brett said.

"I'm excited to go. I hope I'll get to play, or at least hit. I don't think they want me in there (defensively) over Mattingly in the ninth inning."

In one sense, the game counts for nothing. In another sense, for Brett, at this stage of his career, having earned an All-Star berth counts for plenty.

Brett's Bats Are Locked Up

Bob Nightengale
May 10, 1988

George Brett's bats have had a tendency to disappear on the road. So for the last 10 years, Royals equipment manager Al Zych said he has stashed Brett's bats into a trunk that is locked and not re-opened until the next day.

"The only bats I worry about are George's," Zych said. "It was about 10 years ago when George brought four bats to New York, and when we got to Minnesota, there weren't any. It turns out the clubhouse kids stole them all and sold them. We've been locking them up, ever since."

july 25, 1988

by Bob Nightengale

Brett Reinforcing Faith Royals Have in Him

As unfair as it sounds, George Brett's heroics are becoming, well, almost routine these days.

Simply, Brett is producing in the clutch at a phenomenal rate—batting .394 with six homers and 56 RBIs with runners in scoring position.

Most recently, Brett hit a two-run homer with two outs on an 0-2 pitch in the eighth inning that lifted the Royals to a dramatic victory Saturday night over the Yankees.

"We probably do take him for granted," Royals Manager John Wathan said. "You've seen him do it so many times, you expect him to do it every time. You know it's humanly impossible, but that's what you expect.

"I think sometimes when you play (with) the guy and see him every day you can't help but take him for granted. But then you start looking up the numbers of other greats who've played the game, and you're really amazed.

"I still marvel at him all of the time and appreciate it (his feats) more and more. Certainly I can't imagine anyone else I'd rather have at the plate in a crucial situation."

Brett, who has not gone longer than two games without a hit, raised his batting average to .336 Sunday. He also has 16 homers and 73 RBIs and ranks among the league leaders in six offensive categories.

If Brett continues at this pace, he'll finish the season with 27 homers and 122 RBIs. It would give him the highest RBI total of his career.

"If I can keep up what I've done, just stay consistent," Brett said, "to me it would be a tremendous achievement. I think it would have to be considered my best year. I know I'd be more proud of this season than any I've ever had.

"I heard a lot of talk the last two years that my best years were behind me, and to tell you the truth, I wasn't sure if they were right. I didn't know I was capable of having this kind of year."

August 7, 1988

Brett scored the 1,200th run of his career Saturday, coming in on Frank Wills' wild pitch. Then he connected with his 250th home run in the ninth. Last Wednesday, he notched his 7,500th career at-bat. All are Royals' highs.

1988

by Bob Nightengale

Brett Feels He's Back in Stride

George Brett, watching the bright numbers revealing his batting average each night on the scoreboard at Royals Stadium, winced each time it appeared.

For the first four months of the season, Brett had been saying this perhaps might be the best of his 15-year career. Now one lousy month was ruining everything.

"I had no fun last month, no fun at all," said Brett, who hit .228 from August 7 to September 5. "I have fun when we win. I can live with that. But when we lose, I can't live with going 0 for four, one for five."

Brett, playing in front of his brothers Ken and Bobby while his dad watched at home in Southern California, had his first three-hit game since August 20 and only his second since July 27.

"I'm hitting the ball hard again, I'm seeing the ball good, I'm waiting on it good," Brett said. "I'm hitting it with power to left field again, which is always a sign I'm swinging good.

"Just hopefully, I can keep this going for the rest of the season and try to get the average as high as I can, drive in as many runs as I can and help the team win as many games as I can."

Paul Iwanga, Kansas City Star

After a frustrating month in which he hit .228, George Brett was back in the swing of things in September.

1988

october 3, 1988

by Bob Nightengale

Season Brings Brett, Gubicza Renewed Confidence

A sense of urgency burned inside each of them. George Brett was obsessed with trying to re-establish himself as one of the best hitters in the game. Mark Gubicza was driven by the desire to live up to his potential.

In a season of disappointment for the Royals, these two players walked off the field Sunday having fulfilled their individual quests.

Brett—who played his most games, 157, in 13 seasons, hit .306 and drove in 103 runs—silenced his critics and erased his own nagging doubts about his ability.

For Brett, the anguish of missing 85 games the last two seasons weighed heavily on his mind when he went home to Palm Springs, Calif. It was the first time in his career he had batted under .300 in consecutive seasons. And, for the first time, he was doubting his own abilities.

"I heard people saying, 'Yeah, he's old,'" Brett said. "He hasn't taken care of himself. He's washed up. He's not going to be the player he was.'

"I thought a lot about what they said over the winter when I was working out. And I really didn't know myself.

"I certainly didn't go to spring training with all of the confidence in the world, that's for sure. I didn't know what to expect myself.

"The one thing I wanted to do was play as many games as I possibly could. I always thought if I could stay healthy all year long, I could put some impressive numbers on the board. And that's what I did."

Brett opened the season with a home run in his first at-bat and was hitting .350 by mid-May. He was selected to his 13th consecutive All-Star Game, and his first as a first baseman, with his .329 batting average and 61 RBIs.

The only disappointment to his individual accomplishments was his slump the final two months. He was hitting .339 as of August 1 but was unable to maintain the pace and hit .240 the remainder of the season.

"The one thing I was really looking forward to," Brett said, "was that people have always said, 'It doesn't matter what George hits in April and May. When it gets to be June, July, August and September, that's when he really starts swinging the bat good.'

"So I'm sitting there thinking, 'God, if I'm hitting .339 now, how high will I be at the end of the season? Look out (Wade) Boggs; look out Kirby (Puckett); look out (Don) Mattingly.' And it went the opposite way...

"But hey, if someone had told me in spring training my average was going to be .305 with 24 homers and 103 RBIs, I'd take it. So I've got to be happy with the year I've had."

1988

George Brett is what the game of baseball is meant to be.

**—Sparky Anderson,
Detroit Tigers manager**

Brett and teammate Frank White were appointed the first co-captains of the Royals in 1989. Being formally recognized as a leader on the team, Brett began to examine his reputation. He had "grown up" with the Royals, and therefore his private life had been examined by the press. Now a more mature player, Brett's image was slowly changing.

Brett's leadership on the field was cut short by a serious knee injury in April, sidelining him for six weeks. Upon his return, his play suffered and, for the first time in 14 years, George Brett was not selected as an All-Star.

Despite recording the 2,500th hit of his career, Brett's numbers were at an all-time low at the end of the season. A disappointed Brett found himself pondering his future in baseball.

by Bob Nightengale

Brett, White Become First Co-Captains

BASEBALL CITY, Fla.—George Brett and Frank White became the first co-captains of the Royals when Manager John Wathan made the announcement at a team meeting.

The news, which drew an ovation from their teammates, was a surprise because the Royals had not named a captain in their 20-year history.

"Times change, circumstances change," Royals General Manager John Schuerholz said. "Theirs is the essence of what the Royals' organization is all about. It's not only how hard they've worked and how they've represented themselves as professionals, but how they've represented the organization in first-class fashion. In my mind, there is not two more ideal people anywhere in all of baseball."

Brett, 35, the Royals' first baseman, and White, 38, second base, each broke in with the Royals in 1973.

A Big Hit

by Nancy Vessell
January 29, 1989

George Brett proved that he knows how to please the crowd when he addressed the Missouri House this week. Having just appeared before the Senate, the Royals' first baseman played to the competition between the two chambers when he remarked:

"We just left the Senate, and there were two people in there. I'm glad to see someone is working."

That brought cheers, as did his promise to try to bring a World Series to Missouri this year.

1989

by Bob **Nightengale**

Brett Sees Reputation as a Vital Part of Career

BASEBALL CITY, Fla.—At a time when spring training has been dominated by news of Wade Boggs' extramarital affair and Pete Rose's alleged gambling problems, it seems almost unusual to examine a baseball star whose reputation remains intact.

His name is George Brett, a 13-year All-Star, two-time batting champion and career .312 hitter.

Brett's nightlife exploits still are well known in clubhouses throughout baseball, but now at age 35, he is indulging in those activities much less frequently.

Always a hard-worker on the field, Brett appears to be driving himself with even greater effort. When's the last time you heard of a 15-year veteran volunteer for every long road trip of the spring? This spring Brett is the only Royals' player to make the three-hour bus ride to West Palm Beach, the two-hour drive to Clearwater and the two-hour drive to Sarasota.

"Except for the Pine-Tar game, which happened on the field, it's really been a controversy-free career," Brett said the other day. "I just hope I can continue it along those lines.

> **I think my overall image of being a bachelor and going out and enjoying life after the games is overblown. I don't think there's anything wrong with that, as long as I'm able to perform the next day, and I've proven I can do it.**
>
> **—George Brett**

"I'd hate to do something now to tarnish the good image that a few people might still hold of me."

The controversies in Brett's 15 years in Kansas City have been local incidents. In May 1981, Brett hit a UPI photographer on the forehead with his crutch; in September 1981, Brett and a reporter for *The Kansas City Star* and *The Kansas City Times* had to be restrained from fighting, and last March he broke a camera of the publisher of *The Squire* and *The Squire's Other Paper*.

"Those weren't the smartest things I've ever done," Brett said, "but I've had a pretty conservative career as far as getting in trouble.

"I think my overall image of being a bachelor and going out and enjoying life after the games is overblown. I don't think there's anything wrong with that, as long as I'm able to perform the next day, and I've proven I can do it.

"I've also proven with old age that I've changed a little bit, and I don't live the same lifestyle I used to when I was 26 or 27 or 28. I don't do those things that much anymore. I realize the importance of coming to the

1989

ballpark mentally prepared and not hung over or tired from partying all night."

Brett, who will be 36 in May, says he may be more image-conscious than ever. His career has been too successful to allow some stupid incident to ruin 15 years of fan appeal, and he has a genuine concern for the image of the game.

He recognizes the need for role models more than ever, and if he can help the game's image with his behavior, he said he gladly will accept the role as a goodwill ambassador.

His only ground rule is that he refuses to give up his only major vice—chewing tobacco.

"You can meet a lot of good people in this game and have an influence on their lives," Brett said. "And hopefully over the next five years in which I hope to play this game, I can make a good influence on some people.

on your neck.'

"But that's the way I grew up. I knew what was right. I knew what was wrong. Regardless of what other people did, it might be fine in someone else's household, but it wasn't fine in our household. We had rules, and we stuck to the rules.

"I don't see what's so hard about that."

Boston Red Sox outfielder Mike Greenwell confesses unabashedly that at the age of 25, he still has an idol.

"I used to love to watch George Brett play," Greenwell said. "I think it really inspired me to see the way he worked, the way he played, the way he threw himself completely into the game."

There are others like Greenwell, who idolized Brett while growing up and now play on the same level. There's Wade Boggs. There's Mark Ryal. There's David Cone. There's…

I love baseball. I don't know what it is, but there's something about this game that I can't wait to start playing. I must love it, because they say when you're having fun, time flies, and if this is my 16th year, this has really flown by.

"I know I've been a bad influence on some people because I chew tobacco. I get letters every day asking me to stop chewing because of the influence on their children. Hey, it's not my job to raise some kid in South Dakota. It's not my job to raise some kid in Minnesota. And it's not my job to raise this kid in Tuscaloosa. I really don't feel it's my job to raise the kids; it's the parents' job to raise them.

"If I ever came home with an earring in my ear, my dad would rip my ear off—to this day. He wouldn't just rip the earring off, he'd cut my ear off.

"If I ever came home with a tattoo on my arm, he'd cut my arm off. He wouldn't try to erase the tattoo, he'd just cut my arm off. He'd come over to my house with a hatchet when I was sound asleep, and hmph, there it goes. He'd say, 'You're lucky that tattoo wasn't

"It's flattering, really," Brett said, "and kind of embarrassing. I mean, guys like Boggsy (Boggs) are great players, and here they're telling me I'm their idol. I get goosebumps thinking about it."

What it is, really, is a tribute to the way Brett plays. And now, Brett's wish is that the way he carries himself off the field also will be an example.

"I try to go out there and play each game like it's my last game," he said. "Just like last year, I'm going to go out there and try to enjoy it as much as anyone on the field.

"I love baseball. I don't know what it is, but there's something about this game that I can't wait to start playing. I must love it, because they say when you're having fun, time flies, and if this is my 16th year, this has really flown by."

may 10, 1989

by Bob Nightengale

Brett Says Turf Is Culprit for Injury

George Brett vowed the moment he heard the gruesome popping sound in his right knee 10 days ago that he never would play another game on the artificial turf at Royals Stadium.

"I remember the first words I said to them (Royals officials) were, "You can take this turf and stick it up your …,'" Brett said Tuesday. "I said I'll never play on this AstroTurf for the rest of my life."

Brett's frustrations have somewhat eased since that April 29 evening when he suffered a torn medial collateral ligament in his right knee. He says he easily could change his mind by the time he's ready to play in about eight weeks, but as of right now, he refuses to back down from his previous thinking.

"There are a lot of things going through my mind right now, and that's one of them," Brett said. "There are things I still want to accomplish in my career, and if I keep doing this, I'm not going to have a chance to do it."

Brett, who has missed stretches of eight games or more 16 times in his career because of injuries, has had plenty of injuries that are unexplainable, but this one he said can be directly attributed to the artificial turf at Royals Stadium.

The injury occurred when Rob Deer of the Brewers hit a ball into shallow right field, just beyond Brett's reach. Brett caught the ball

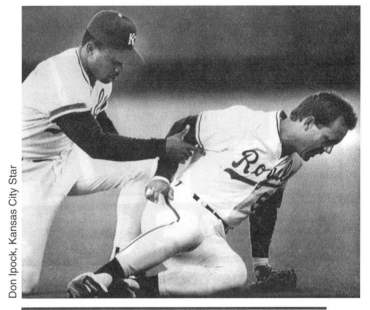

Don Ipock, Kansas City Star

Kansas City Royals right fielder Danny Tartabull helps injured teammate George Brett during the top of the first inning. Brett was injured while chasing a ball hit by Milwaukee's Rob Deer.

on one bounce, but when he spun to make a throw, his spikes got caught in the turf as he released the ball.

He is undergoing therapy each day to make sure atrophy does not result, but Brett said he has no idea when he'll return. It could be six more weeks. It could be eight more weeks. It could be even longer.

by Jonathan Rand

Royals Begin to Show That They Miss Brett

DETROIT—At first, the Royals overcame the absence of George Brett the way the Oakland Athletics shrugged off the loss of injured Jose Canseco.

They kept winning.

Even without Brett, who suffered a torn medial collateral ligament in his right knee April 29 against Milwaukee, the Royals won 11 of 16 and were tied for first place in the American League West as recently as last Tuesday.

But a season-most four-game losing streak, including a 4-2 loss to Detroit on Sunday, has underscored how much the Royals miss Brett.

They're not hitting. They're not producing runs. And they've fallen into third place in the American League West, 3 $\frac{1}{2}$ games out.

The Royals are 11-9 without Brett, largely because of a pitching staff that has kept the team in games and has lowered its ERA from 3.38 to 3.09 in those 20 games.

"We can't keep holding teams to one or two runs or no runs," said Royals Manager John Wathan. "We need a key hit in a key situation with runners on to get out of this."

Indeed, the Royals were one for 21 with runners in scoring position and left 24 men on base in the three losses to Detroit.

Aside from a two-night binge in Minnesota last week, the offense has taken a dramatic dip since Brett has been out.

Before Brett was hurt, the Royals were hitting .265 as a team and were averaging 5.09 runs and 9.1 hits per game. In the 20 games Brett has missed, the Royals are hitting .238, and averaging only 2.9 runs and 7.8 hits.

Though Brett was hitting only .253, he had 13 RBIs, which still is tied for fourth on the team. Before he was hurt, the Royals were 63 for 203 (.310) with 88 RBIs when they had runners in scoring position. In the 20 games without Brett, they are 29 for 130 (.223) with 41 RBIs with runners in scoring position.

Before and After

The Brett Factor

Before Injury		*After
22	Games	20
.265	Average	.238
758	At-bats	660
112	Runs	59
201	Hits	157
41	Doubles	16
2	Triples	3
13	Home Runs	25
103	Runs Batted In	57
85	Walks	65
105	Strikeouts	122
37	Stolen Bases	20
14-8	Record	11-9

*Includes game April 29 when Brett was hurt in the top of the first inning.

by Mike Fish

Brett Takes the Break with Mixed Emotions

For the first time in 14 years, George Brett, now 36, can relax during an All-Star break. There is no game to play, no bows to take. Just three days of relaxation and golf at the Lake of the Ozarks.

"I wanted to go again," said Brett, who grew up 45 minutes from Anaheim Stadium, site of this year's All-Star Game. "Obviously my numbers aren't good enough to go. But if I had my choice, I would go. I always had a good time going to those things."

No active player has a longer streak than Brett—13 years. But after being sidelined six weeks because of a knee injury and scuffling offensively after his return, Brett harbored no false hopes.

The major disappointment is not returning to Southern California as an All-Star. In 1980, the last time the game was contested on his home turf, Brett didn't play at Dodger Stadium because of an injury.

"Next year is Wrigley Field (in Chicago)," Brett said. "That's a place I've never played. I'd love to come back and play there next year."

His first appearance came at the 1976 game in Philadelphia. Brett was elected to the starting lineup every season through 1986. The last two seasons he was selected as a reserve, including last season as a first baseman.

In 1976, Brett was only in his third season and succeeded Graig Nettles of the New York Yankees. At the time, he was better known as the younger brother of Ken Brett, winning pitcher in the 1974 All-Star Game.

"One thing I remember is they did the introductions before the game for the television cameras," Bobby Brett said. "They had the guys lined up and he says, 'Hi, I'm George Brett of the Kansas City Royals. I'm Ken Brett's baby brother.'"

Brett's Past Injuries

1977:	Missed 13 games because of injury to right elbow
1978:	Missed 33 games because of two injuries to left shoulder
1980:	Missed 44 games because of injuries to right heel, right ankle and right hand
1982:	Missed 12 games because of injury to right wrist
1983:	Missed 22 games because of injury to left toe
1984:	Missed 53 games because of injuries to left knee and left hamstring
1985:	Missed eight games because of injury to right hamstring
1986:	Missed 42 games because of two injuries to right shoulder
1987:	Missed 44 games because of injuries to ribs and right knee
1989:	Placed on 21-day disabled list because of injury to right knee

by The Kansas City Star

Brett Gets 2,500th Hit, Knocks in Run with Single

Ed Rode, Kansas City Star

Royals first baseman George Brett recorded the 2,500th hit of his major-league career Friday night when he singled to center in the third inning of the Royals' 6-0 victory over Minnesota.

Brett received a handshake from Twins first baseman Kent Hrbek and tipped his cap to the crowd. The ball was retrieved and tossed to Brett, who gave it to first-base coach Bob Schaefer.

"Hrbek told me, 'Congratulations, old timer,'" Brett said.

Brett said he was prepared for the occasion.

"I really anticipated it happening to-night," he said. "I got a lot of calls from friends all over the country today saying, 'Tonight is the night. I'll be looking for you on Sports Center.'"

Royals first baseman George Brett acknowledges the crowd after getting his 2,500 hit.

Sore Arm Keeps Brett on Bench

by Dick Kaegel
September 5, 1989

DETROIT—George Brett, his right arm still hurting, missed the Royals' game Monday.

Brett has not yet played a game this season at Tiger Stadium, where the Royals are 0-4. This is one of Brett's favorite parks; he has hit 16 homers here.

Brett said he was having difficulty twisting the arm, which was bruised below the elbow when he was hit by a pitch Sunday in Texas.

1989

september 9, 1989

by Steve Cameron

Brett Sets His Sights on 3,000 Hits

To set the record straight, George Brett did not get a hit on the first major-league pitch he saw.

No, he crashed a line drive straight back at Chicago pitcher Stan Bahnsen, who got his glove up and snared the ball just in time to prevent serious dental damage.

"My first hit was the next at-bat, on a broken-bat single to left," recalled Brett, throwing back his head to laugh. "Charley Lau said, 'I like that stroke.'"

The little business with Bahnsen occurred August 2, 1973, in Comiskey Park. Perhaps the White Sox pitcher has never forgotten Brett's debut, if only because his facial features were put at risk.

But the rest of the baseball world took scant notice. Scouts did not fall from their seats, eyes popping, predicting that Brett would stand at first base in 1989, waving to an adoring crowd, celebrating his 2,500th hit.

That happy occasion took place Friday, but Brett recalled how insignificant those early at-bats were considered.

"It's not like I got a hit and started dreaming about 2,500 or 3,000 or anything," he said. "My goal back then was to keep from going back to Omaha. The meal money down there was $4 a day."

In fact, Brett lasted 12 days in the big show. He was back in Nebraska on August 14.

"I don't think people remember that," said Brett, who was recalled in September that first year and wound up hitting a lusty .125. "After my first hit, my only goal was No. 2. Then No. 3. I started the next year at Omaha, too, you know."

This was not a player with huge aspirations.

"I never hit .300 in the minors," he said. "When I first signed, my brother invested my signing bonus and I really thought I'd play three to five years in the minors, and that would be it."

But Brett came to Kansas City for good on May 3, 1974, hit .282 and began drilling the seemingly endless succession of line drives which someday could take him to the Hall of Fame.

Let's dispatch another matter right off: Yes, Brett, 36, intends to swing away for 3,000 hits and, good health permitting, says he'll get there.

"If I hadn't had so many injuries, the six-week or two-month kind," Brett said, "I might not be too far from 3,000 already.

"But hopefully, in another three or three and a half years, I'll get there. I'd like to get 'em all in a Royals uniform."

Never in my wildest dreams did I ever think I'd win a batting title this year. I thought my career was over four or five months ago.

—George Brett

Brett stunned fans everywhere in early 1990 by stating in an interview that he wanted to be traded if the Royals refused to grant him a richer contract. Almost immediately, he regretted his comments when he was bombarded by the press with questions and concerns. Brett blamed his statements on temporary frustrations and said, "It wasn't one of the smartest things I've ever done. I said it in the heat of battle."

In the wake of controversy, Brett had a slow start, going one for 18. He was excluded from the All-Star selections, and by midseason the Royals were near the bottom of the division.

After the All-Star break, however, Brett snapped out of his slump and brought his average up over .300. Suddenly, he was involved in the AL batting race.

Brett's miracle season ended in triumph when he became the first player in major-league history to win batting titles in each of three decades. He was also voted Royals Player of the Year by the Kansas City Chaper of the Baseball Writers Association of America.

by Steve Cameron

Brett Demands Richer Contract—or Trade

Royals superstar George Brett stunned his employers, teammates and fans alike on Tuesday with a sharply worded demand for a richer contract.

Brett's remarks, which became public after an interview with the *Spokane (Wash.) Spokesman-Review*, included a suggestion that he should be traded if the Royals would not renegotiate his current deal of $1.5 million per year.

Brett signed a so-called lifetime deal in 1984, an arrangement that includes a $1.5 million salary through 1991 with options for two years beyond that. Real-estate deals and other considerations were included that would keep Brett on the Royals' payroll indefinitely.

But Brett, 36, apparently has been chafing over huge salaries being paid to players without records approaching his own. So last Friday, in a business trip to Spokane, Brett made his demands known to the *Spokesman-Review*, which printed the story Tuesday morning.

"I understand that, yeah, I did sign a contract," Brett was quoted as saying. "I've got to play out that contract, and I will honor that contract, but right now I'm not looking forward to going to spring training unless my attitude changes."

Brett characterized his relationship with the Royals as shaky and said the contract problems were disturbing his off-season conditioning routine.

Brett Regrets Making Contract Comments

**by Mike DeArmond
January 31, 1990**

George Brett walked out of his morning shower today into the thunderstorm of controversy he knew he had created and discussed the possibility that he had lost his mind.

Brett said he really started to have second thoughts about what he had said to the reporter after his conversation with Royals General Manager John Schuerholz made him feel better about his personal situation with the club, and that he tried to stop publication of the story.

"When I talked to that guy I was at that boiling point where everything is just blown so far out of proportion that I had to get it off my chest," Brett said. "I called the guy the day that it happened to come out in the paper. I said: 'Please don't put that article in the paper.' It was too late. It went in that day. Now I have to live with it."

by Jack Etkin

Brett Tries to Forget His 1-for-18 Start

Though hitless in his last 11 at-bats and mired at .056, he says, "I know what I'm doing wrong."

At a time like this, when George Brett says, "Instead of getting better, it's getting worse," he has summoned up some timeless wisdom from his hitting mentor.

"It's like Charley Lau used to say," Brett said, "even when you're swinging the worst you've ever swung, you've got to try and manufacture one hit a day. You've got to get that one a day. That's what I'm trying to do.

"I thought I had one today. I'm not going to start begging for them. If they come, they come. If not …."

So far they haven't. Brett was hitless in four at-bats Saturday in the Royals' 3-1 victory over the Toronto Blue Jays. His bottom line for the young season: one hit—a single grounded up the middle—in 18 at-bats for an .056 average.

Since that single against Baltimore's Jeff Ballard in the first inning Wednesday, Brett has gone hitless in his last 11 at-bats and failed to hit the ball out of the infield in his last eight.

"I know what I'm doing wrong," Brett said. "I'm just having a tough time correcting it. I'm pulling off everything, and I'm not going to hit if I pull off everything. Every time I go up there and tell myself, 'Don't pull off, don't pull off.' And I pull off."

Brett Likely to Move to Right Field

by Steve Cameron
May 18, 1990

NEW YORK—George Brett has fond memories of the right-field seats at Yankee Stadium.

He's likely to see them up close this weekend.

Royals Manager John Wathan said Thursday that Brett is the logical candidate to play right field since slugger Danny Tartabull is coming off the disabled list and is likely to be designated hitter.

"We want to keep as many good bats in the lineup as possible, so I talked to George about playing some right field. We could keep (designated hitter) Gerald Perry in there at first and George in the outfield until Danny is healthy enough to play defense."

by Jack Etkin

All-Star Break Brings Odd Times for Brett

George Brett could have been part of the All-Star scene. The opportunity was there to play golf at Medinah Country Club, site of the U.S. Open last month, and even keep his pact with Royals trainer Mickey Cobb.

"Every time he went to the All-Star Game," Brett said, "I was supposed to go with him."

That was the agreement they reached in 1982, when both were at the All-Star Game in Montreal. Cobb will be in the American League dugout tonight at Wrigley Field in Chicago. Brett had the chance to be nearby. A company he would prefer not to identify would have seen to that. The demands weren't going to be much.

"I was invited to go and golf with their clients and sit at the game and go to cocktail parties beforehand," Brett said, "but that's not what I want to do. I just don't want to be a spectator at an All-Star Game while I'm still active. I'm sure when I'm through playing, I would like to go and see some of them."

Brett knows exactly what would have happened had he accepted the corporate invitation. How awkward it would have been. One question would have been repeated.

"'How come you're not playing?' Well, when I get retired or get released then it's easy to say, 'Hey, I'm no longer a player. I'm just here as a fan,'" he said.

Brett Says He Has Come Too Far to Settle for Division Cellar

July 12, 1990

BALTIMORE—Message to the fans of Kansas City from George Brett:

"I guarantee you we're not going to be a last-place ballclub," the Royals' first baseman said Wednesday night.

"I think we'll have a big second half. We may not win it, but we won't finish last. I've been in the big leagues 17 years and never been last, and I won't be this year, either."

"I know the fans at home are frustrated," he said. "They've seen good-quality performances for so many years and now they aren't.

"But I promise you the fans can't possibly be as frustrated as the players are."

1990

by Dick Kaegel

Brett's Sweet Swing and Hall of Fame Numbers Return

BALTIMORE—A retired baseball writer from the *Baltimore Sun* ambled into the Royals' clubhouse Saturday and found George Brett.

"You've got my vote for the Hall of Fame, George," Jim Elliot said. "Even if you retire tomorrow."

Brett, with a career of rich achievements, would seem to be a logical choice five years after he retires.

"When people mention it like that gentleman did, obviously it's quite a compliment, but, to be honest, I never, ever think about it," Brett said.

It's kind of a weird situation. You kind of control your own destiny, but you have no control over it. If I go out and hit .300 three more years, yeah, that will definitely help my chances. If I get 3,000 hits, that's definitely going to help my chances. But I don't make that decision."

Brett has rediscovered the classic swing that, before this season, had given him a .310 career average and 10 years over the .300 mark topped by his .390 in 1980.

It's a bubbly Brett these days, contrasted to the frequently flat personality that inhabited the Royals' clubhouse earlier this year.

When you're the third-spot hitter on a club picked to contend and, on May 7, you're batting .200 and the club is dead last, there's no joy in Mudville.

Brett has thought a lot about what went wrong.

"It was a little bit of mechanics and, I think, a lot in my head. I let the mechanics get to me. I let the slow start of the team make me, like everybody else, try to do things I wasn't capable of doing," he said.

Brett Moves to Top in AL Batting Race

September 18, 1990

George Brett is leading the American League in hitting. He rested Monday against Minnesota and kept his average at .3254 while Oakland's Rickey Henderson went hitless in two at-bats against Chicago and fell to .3251. And Rafael Palmeiro went five-for-five for Texas against Seattle, raising his average to .3247.

All of the averages round to .325, but Brett would win the title if the season were over.

october 4, 1990

by Jack Etkin

Hit Makes History for Brett

A season that began so ruinously for George Brett that he drifted into self-doubt ended in triumph Wednesday when he won his third American League batting title and made baseball history.

With a sacrifice fly and single in the Royals' 5-2 defeat in Cleveland, officially a one-for-one game, Brett finished with a .329 average. He and Rickey Henderson of the Oakland Athletics dueled in the waning days of the season, jockeying for position by playing intermittently. Henderson went one-for-three Wednesday and ended with an average of .325.

"It's absolutely crazy to be so bad for long and turn it around and be written off and come back the way I did," Brett said at Kansas City International Airport after the Royals'

> It's absolutely crazy to be so bad for long and turn it around and be written off and come back the way I did. Never in my wildest dreams did I ever think I'd win a batting title this year. I thought my career was over four or five months ago.
> —George Brett

charter landed. "Never in my wildest dreams did I ever think I'd win a batting title this year. I thought my career was over four or five months ago."

On May 7, Brett was batting .200. Eight days later, he turned 37 and was still burdened with a .234 average. As late as June 30, Brett's average was a modest .256.

When play resumed July 11 after the All-Star break, Brett had a three-hit game at Baltimore and the start of a sizzling stretch. In the season's second half, Brett hit .388, pounding out 108 hits in 278 at-bats.

"There was just so much doubt in myself early on in the season," Brett said. "I really doubted my ability. I don't anymore."

1990

december 1, 1990

by Dick Kaegel

It's Unanimous: Brett is Royals' Player of the Year

George Brett says his third batting title has earned him more toasts than any previous achievement. "I've gotten more congratulations from this than I did the year I almost hit .400," he said Friday.

There is another round of handshakes and applause ahead. Brett has been selected the Royals' Player of the Year by the Kansas City Chapter of the Baseball Writers Association of America.

Brett was a unanimous choice—no surprise, since his bid to become the first player to win batting titles in three decades provided a shining light in the Royals' dark season.

"Everywhere I go, every flight I've been on, the captain wants to meet you ... the stewardess gives you a bottle of champagne ... 'My husband and I were following you, happy to see you win' ... 'Here's a bottle of champagne from the crew,'" Brett said.

He's received a stack of congratulatory letters, ranging from Oakland Manger Tony La Russa to a former Babe Ruth roommate, Jimmie Reese.

Joe Ledford, Kansas City Star

After winning his third batting title in three decades, Brett was the unanimous choice as the Royals' Player of the Year.

Joe Ledford, Kansas City Star

He's the old man of the Royals, but in some ways, George Brett never seemed younger. He still smiles. His wildly unmanageable hair is still blond. He remains the glamour boy of his team, still Kansas City's favorite athletic son.

—Mike Eisenbath
St. Louis Post-Dispatch

A Veteran Stumbles

Brett cruised through the spring of 1991 but was forced off the field with a partial tear of the medial collateral ligament in his right knee in April. Although he was frustrated at the thought of missing more than 300 games because of injuries thus far in his career, Brett remained fairly optimistic about his future in baseball.

After his climb back from injury, Brett slowly made his way to 2,800 hits. His average had its ups and downs, but at the end of the season he was far from satisfied. Brett had endured a year that was perhaps the worst in his 18-year career and that included "a period when my performance was so bad, it just wore me down mentally."

march 17, 1991

by Dick Kaegel

Brett Stays on Spring Tear with Winning 3-Run Blast

1991

BASEBALL CITY, Fla.—George Brett's torrid spring continued Saturday in chilly Florida. Brett slammed a three-run homer off left-hander Tom Browning as the Royals defeated the Cincinnati Reds 4-2 in a game called after $4\frac{1}{2}$ innings because of rain. That gave Brett nine hits in 15 at-bats (.600) with two homers and seven RBIs. His 15 total bases puts his slugging percentage at 1.000.

"It's a good confidence booster," Brett said.

Brett's homer to right field came in the third inning after singles by Gary Thurman and Kevin Seitzer.

"We've had a lot of batting practice against the coaches—more than ever—and that helps," Brett said. "I've spent a lot of time in the cages, too, and you can get a lot of fundamental work done there."

Manager John Wathan said: "He's on fire this spring. I hope that's an indication of a quick start in 1991. A hot George Brett in April would help make a good start for us, that's for sure."

Bret Saberhagen pitched four innings for the victory, allowing seven hits and two runs (one earned).

"I didn't have too good of a curve, but my change-up was good, and my arm felt good," Saberhagen said.

There was none of the shoulder stiffness that bothered him earlier this spring.

"It's kind of scary," he said. "It feels too good."

It was the third time in this damp spring that a Royals game was shortened by rain. A game with the Chicago White Sox was called off after three innings. The Royals won an earlier game with the Reds in $5\frac{1}{2}$ innings.

The Royals have a 3-5-1 record.

april 24, 1991

by Dick Kaegel

Brett Won't Play Again for a Month

Ligament Tear Is Latest Setback

CLEVELAND—George Brett's voice sounded flat and somber over the phone line from Kansas City.

"I'm lying here," he said, "with a splint on my leg."

Never mind the severe pain in his right knee. The pain in his voice spoke volumes.

When Brett can't play baseball, he hurts inside, too.

He is not expected to play again for a month. He got that news late Tuesday afternoon after an examination in Kansas City.

Brett, the Royals' first baseman, suffered a partial tear of the medial collateral ligament in his right knee in Monday night's game at Cleveland Stadium. And, while the Royals were preparing Tuesday to play the second game of the three-game series against the Indians, Brett was on his back in his Kansas City house.

"This is getting old when you tear your ligaments three times in your right knee and twice in your left," Brett said wearily.

The medial collateral ligament also was torn April 29, 1989, and Brett missed 35 games.

That tear, however, was below the joint line; this one is above it. The same knee was injured in 1987, costing him 24 games.

Brett has missed more than 300 games because of injuries since 1977.

Throughout his career, Brett was sidelined five times by knee injuries.

Joe Ledford, Kansas City Star

1991

by Jack Etkin

Brett Not Thinking The End Is Near

The results are eerily familiar. George Brett was rising from the hitting depths a year ago, just as he is now, albeit with one nagging question happily missing:

Am I done?

"I have never felt that this year," Brett said.

He asked that question of himself long and hard in 1990. Brett was hitting .200 on May 7 and, as he said, leading the league in pop flies to left and ground balls to second base. Vying with Rickey Henderson for the batting title and winning it with a .329 average were pipe dreams when spring was turning to summer.

And why not? Brett was coming off a .282 season in 1989 and reached that level only because he hit .341 after August 9.

"Last year with the slow start," Brett said, "I was wondering if the second half of '89 was my last little get-up-and-let's-get-it-in-gear run because it just didn't seem like things were getting better."

After going zero-for-four in Thursday night's 3-2 victory over Baltimore, Brett is hitting .253 with 11 doubles, two homers and 21 RBIs.

On this date last season, Brett was at .259 with nine doubles, one homer and 20 RBIs. He had played in 59 games, compared with 38 this season because of a knee injury that put him on the disabled list from April 23 to May 23.

"Last year it seemed like I never saw the ball," Brett said, "and I never got a good swing off. It was a real consistent inconsistency. I was out in front of everything or behind everything.

"This year on opening day I got hits off (Greg) Swindell and (Jesse) Orosco, both lefties, and hit the ball hard every time but one. I'm going, 'Yeah, I'm in that groove.'"

He played just 11 more games before leaving the lineup and could ponder a six-for-43 (.140) stretch after jump-starting the season with that two-hit opener. Mulling his misfortune at being hurt, though undoubtedly gloomy, he was positively upbeat compared with wondering whether the end had abruptly arrived.

"I have never felt that this year," Brett said. "(I was) struggling with my swing early. But there were very few at-bats. Didn't panic. Didn't feel it was over. I just felt I was struggling. Every day it was something different.

"One day I wouldn't see the ball. The next day I saw the ball good and just took bad swings at it."

1991

I nductees George Brett (right) and Len Dawson (left) were joined by Special Olympian Donald Hudson (center) on the Kansas City Walk of Stars. Smaller stars below the star for each athlete bear the name of a Special Olympian.

by Dick Kaegel

Brett Sends Club on Way to Cleveland with Blast

11th-inning Homer Caps a Four-Hit Day

MILWAUKEE—When George Brett headed for the plate to lead off the 11th inning Thursday, Royals Manager Hal McRae had a devilish thought.

"Put a good swing on it, Mullet," McRae told him, "because I know you always have so much fun in Cleveland."

Brett gave McRae a double take.

"Say w-h-a-t?"

Brett may not have been in any hurry to get to Cleveland but he did want this long game with the Milwaukee Brewers to end happily.

With that, he lined a 2-1 pitch from Brewers reliever Darren Holmes over the left-field wall, breaking a 4-4 tie. The Royals added another run in the inning and won 6-5.

That climaxed a four-hit day for Brett, his second of the year. His seventh homer raised his average to .270, his high for the season.

"Naw, I was .500 on opening day, two for four," Brett said.

OK, and he was at .333 after the third game and .294 after the fourth game.

The point is Brett's average plummeted thereafter to .170, then he missed 26 games because of a knee injury. Since his return, it's been a slow but steady climb to those additional 100 points.

Brett hit .284 in July and now his August is off to a four-for-six start.

"I felt good yesterday, too," he said after Thursday's victory. "Went one-for-five and hit into three double plays. But I hit the ball hard four times and only got one hit. Today I hit the ball hard two times and got four.

"But I'm feeling better. I know what I've been doing wrong and it's starting to correct itself through early hitting and just concentration, I think." It is a matter, he said, of holding back a bit longer with the upper half of his body before launching into a pitch.

The Royals reached the .500 mark in their 100th game and, with a 12-3 record in the last 15 games, Brett senses a positive attitude.

"It's been an uphill struggle, I know that," he said. "Hopefully, we can get something working in the next 62 ballgames."

"The main thing now is when we walk out on the field, we feel we have a chance to beat the other team. That always helps. You go out there for the National Anthem and there's that feeling of 'Hey, we can beat these guys.' Rather than before it was 'Well, how are we going to lose tonight?'"

Oh, and Brett's really not that down on Cleveland anymore.

"It's a lot better than it used to be," he said.

So is his batting average.

1991

august 18, 1991

by Dick Kaegel

Brett's Two Doubles Give Him 2,800 Hits

BOSTON—Hit No. 3,000 is just 200 away for George Brett.

Brett had two doubles Saturday and raised his career total of hits to 2,800. Brett's goal is to reach 3,000 next season, his 20th with the Royals.

Brett doubled into the left-field corner in the first inning and sent a fly ball to the wall in left in the eighth.

The 34,009 Fenway Park fans gave him a rousing ovation.

"That was great, it really was," Brett said. "For some reason the fans here have been very friendly to me. I don't know if it's because my brother Ken played here and was in a World Series with them or what … But it was a very warm sensation."

Brett's 2,800 total ranks 33rd on the all-time hit list. Only 16 players have 3,000 hits.

He is 12 hits from catching George Sisler, Hall of Fame first baseman for the St. Louis Browns.

At the moment, however, Brett is not pleased with his hitting.

He entered Saturday's game against the Red Sox with just four hits in 33 at-bats (.121).

His average, which had crested at .280 in the game before that stretch, is down to .268.

"It's frustrating a little bit, but you've just got to keep hacking," he said.

Brett's two doubles gave him 1,006 extra-base hits, passing Hall of Famer Honus Wagner for the 18th spot on the all-time list.

Passing Wagner, a big shortstop in the ancient days of the Pittsburgh Pirates, doesn't interest Brett much.

But when he learned he was just one behind Mickey Mantle in the total-bases category (4,511 to 4,510), his eyes lit up.

Mantle is still around, a "colorful" figure as Brett put it, and a guy his father, Jack, used to watch in Yankee Stadium.

"Everybody's heard of Mickey Mantle, on and off the field, and when you start getting mentioned with his name, it's kind of exciting," Brett said.

"I'm not taking anything away from those other guys, but they played 50 or 60 years earlier. But to match total bases with a guy like Mickey Mantle, that's kind of big.

"Mickey Mantle is a legend to people in my era and my father's era."

by Jack Etkin

Brett Finds Little Satisfaction in Subpar Season at the Plate

Royals Star Says Knee Injury Is No Excuse for His Performance

T he theory about his troublesome knee causing his hitting woes seems reasonable.

George Brett just isn't buying it.

He will carry a .258 average into the Royals' game with the California Angels at 9:35 tonight, put the worst season in his 18-year career behind him Sunday and leave the rationalizing to others.

"I've had knee problems before, and I've overcome them with the same amount of rehab," Brett said. "I don't want to use it as an excuse for a very subpar season. I'm not going to use it as an excuse."

On April 22, in the 12th game of the season, Brett tore the medial collateral ligament in his right knee. When he returned May 24, it was with a large brace on that knee.

The left-handed-hitting Brett strides with his right leg, so if it's not as strong as it should be, an incomplete weight transfer can cause other hitting fundamentals to go awry. As Royals Manager Hal McRae said, "being able to get over his leg would allow him to get his hands through the ball."

Brett has immense respect for McRae's knowledge of hitting and said "maybe there's some valid points to what he's saying, I really don't know. It's just that he had two prior operations on each knee and, until this year, had never hit below .282.

"So I can't say this one's different," Brett said. "I think I wasn't using my lower body the way I have in the past. I was a little bit afraid. But I felt strong at the end of the year. The brace is to a point now where I don't know I have it on half the time."

If all goes well, Brett may be able to scrap that brace next season. Before leaving for California next month, Brett will receive an exercise program from Royals trainer Nick Swartz to build the muscles in his upper and lower legs.

"For next year," Swartz said, "the goal is to get the (right) leg strong and maintain strength and go to a lighter sleeve with metal side-bars in it."

In which case, Brett, strictly a designated hitter since May 24, might play first base two or three days a week, a possibility that holds both inherent appeal and risk.

"I think I'd be a better player, but at the same time, I don't want to go through another knee injury," Brett said. "When I get together with Nick, I'm going to maybe see (team physician) Steve Joyce and say, 'Steve, what should I do?'

"Next year I'll be 39 years old, and I've had five knee injuries already. The next one might be the big one. I've never injured my anterior cruciate in my right knee, but my anterior cruciate's real loose right now, and that's why I wear an anterior cruciate brace. And if you tear that, you're out a year minimum. At this point, that's the end of my career."

Brett can reach a career milestone next season: 3,000 hits. Only 16 players in the history of the game have attained that summit. Brett, with 2,836, is likely to be No. 18, following Milwaukee's Robin Yount, who has 2,875. If Brett, with 129 hits in 129 games during this down year, can play 150-155 games in 1992, he thinks he'll reach 3,000 next season. While the arithmetic makes sense, this season brought Brett the gloomy realization that climbing to 3,000 could pit pride against history.

"I played with Harmon Killebrew in his last year," Brett said. "I played with Vada Pinson in his last year. I played with Tommy Davis, Orlando Cepeda and Gaylord Perry in their last years. These were all great players when I was growing up. Now I'm their teammate, and I remember to score Harmon from second base, you had to hit a triple or a ground-rule double.

"I said I never want to get in a position like that. What I did this year is not acceptable to me. I couldn't play like this much longer."

Brett has endured a season that included "a period when my performance was so bad, it just wore me down mentally."

He will be thinking of future promise, not past torment when he begins working out in the off-season. There will be times when he is tired and thinking of cutting short a workout or even skipping an exercise session entirely, and Brett knows then that 3,000 hits will come to mind.

"Johnny Bench quit the game when he was 35 years old," Brett said. "He's a neighbor of mine in California. I asked him one time why he quit. He said, 'I wasn't the player I wanted to be, and I've accomplished everything I wanted to accomplish.' Well, I know I'm not the player I once was, but I haven't accomplished everything I set out to accomplish."

AP/Wide World Photos

B rett finished the season disappointed with his performance. "What I did this year is not acceptable to me," he said.

Joe Ledford, Kansas City Star

It was big here. Sort of the sporting equivalent of a moon landing or an earthquake. George Brett's 3,000th hit held us spellbound one minute and shook us the next. But then, that was expected. Brett is Kansas City's very own technological wonder and natural phenomenon, rolled into one.

—Gib Twyman of *The Kansas City Star*

17

1992

3000!

For George Brett, 1992 was a remarkable year.

In February, Kansas City's "most eligible bachelor" became ineligible when George married Leslie Davenport.

Still a beaming newlywed, Brett found himself in a major batting slump early in the season. He slowly overcame it, and in June he got hit No. 2,900. With 100 hits to go and only 88 games remaining, the chase was on for 3,000.

Ignoring a shoulder injury that had bothered him for the previous 48 hours, Brett belted out four hits in a late September game at Anaheim and reached the historic 3,000 mark. "Nobody knew if he'd even play," Manager Hal McRae said. "And then he gets four hits. That is greatness."

by The Kansas City Star

Sun Comes Out Just in Time for Wedding

Brett and Bride Had Hectic Week

BASEBALL CITY, Fla.—George Brett and Leslie Davenport have been married for a dozen days now.

"And they said it wouldn't last," Brett said, grinning.

Brett, one of the game's most eligible bachelors, kept details of his February 15 wedding in California secret to avoid the glare of publicity. It was a small affair.

"Her immediate family, my immediate family," Brett said. "It comes out to 29. We had it at my brother Bobby's house in Manhattan Beach."

"It's rained for four days and at 3:30 the sun came out. We got married inside the house, but it made it a lot prettier with the sunset in the background because he's got a big house on the ocean there. The best man was my nephew, Kemer's kid Casey, $4\frac{1}{2}$, and the maid of honor was his twin sister, Sheridan."

"Kemer" is brother Ken Brett, a former Royals pitcher.

George Brett and his wife, Leslie, relax in their home.

Tammy Ljungblad, Kansas City Star

1992

april 25, 1992

by Jeffrey **Flanagan**

Is Brett's Slump Over? Who Knows?

TORONTO—Who knows?

That was George Brett's stock answer to every question volleyed at him after the Royals' 4-3 loss Friday night to Toronto.

Brett had just ended a one-for-38 rut with a two-run blast off Tom Henke in the ninth, but frankly, Brett wasn't about to draw any stirring conclusions regarding his second homer of the season.

Did the homer indicate any positive signs?

"Who knows?" Brett said.

Did the three-run rally in the ninth hold any special meaning despite yet another loss?

"Who knows?"

Didn't Brett feel any personal relief from the homer?

"Who knows?"

Finally, after three or four more questions, Brett relented.

"Seriously, it has to get old for you guys (reporters) to come in here every night and try to find something new to ask," Brett said. "Imagine what it's like to find something new every night to answer. Especially when you're one for 15.

"I think 'Who knows?' just about says it all at this point."

And, coincidentally, can you guess what Toronto Manager Cito Gaston had to say about Brett's homer?

"Who knows?" Gaston said. "Maybe we got George out of his slump."

Seriously.

Joe Ledford, Kansas City Star

Brett warms up before taking batting practice.

by Jack Etkin

Brett Seeks Return to Top Hitting Form

The numbers seemed absurdly low to George Brett, too meager to ever serve as goals.

Royals Manager Hal McRae, explaining that carrying the team was no longer Brett's burden, told him in spring training that hitting .270 with, say, 12 home runs and 70 RBIs would be just fine.

"I told him I could do better than that," Brett said, chuckling. "Maybe he knew what he was talking about.

"I really haven't contributed and pulled my share of the load. Hopefully, I can do that before too long."

Brett is hitting .221 with two home runs and eight RBIs. He had one white-hot stretch, followed by an utterly barren period that finally gave way to something nondescript, not vintage Brett but acceptable.

He began the season going seven for 16. He had hits in his first five games, including a three-for-three game April 10 in Seattle, where the Royals finished their first road trip.

"I think I played 11 games in the home stand and got one hit," Brett said, "and this is a park that's been very good to me over the years.

"It's hard to tell what happened. I felt I was swinging the bat decently, good enough to get hits. I just wasn't getting any. Probably panicked a little bit. Got a little frustrated. Got a little down. Ended up digging a pretty big hole to come out of."

Brett's average sank to .157 when the Royals' first home stand ended April 23, enduring a one-for-38 slump. In his last 14 games, Brett has hit .283 (15 for 53), not bad for most players but 25 points below his lifetime average.

Brett will turn 39 Friday and finds himself bouncing over rough terrain. It is the same journey over unforgiving territory that McRae once made. In 1982, McRae, at age 37, hit .308 with 27 home runs and a league-leading 133 RBIs because of maximum mental effort.

Brett needs 141 hits to reach 3,000, something only 16 players have achieved. The Royals have 142 games left. The mathematics are possible this season, certainly by early in 1993, but simply hanging on isn't the way Brett wants to arrive at 3,000.

"It would be fun to do," Brett said. "It would be a tremendous honor and tremendous thrill, but I'm not going to jeopardize 18 good years of baseball to try to achieve something and hurt the organization at the same time."

His roots in the organization go back to 1971, when he went off to play in Billings, Mont., where the Royals had a Class A team in the Pioneer League. Three years later, Brett left the minors for good and joined the Royals.

1992

Joe Ledford, Kansas City Star

A fter a slow start to the 1992 season, Brett was ready to get back on track.

october 1, 1992

by Dick Kaegel

3000, by George!

Brett's Hit Parade Reaches Milestone

ANAHEIM, Calif.—Leave it to George Brett to do the improbable. He always has.

George Brett, after missing two games with a shoulder injury, banged out four hits Wednesday night and reached the historic 3,000 mark.

Brett, the heart and soul of the Royals, became only the 18th player to achieve 3,000 hits.

The milestone hit came in the seventh inning, a one-hop single that rocketed over California Angels second baseman Ken Oberkfell.

Brett couldn't really define his emotions minutes after the game.

"It's really hard to say. My mind's going too fast right now. If I had a beer in my hand, I'd probably be able to do it very easily.

"It happened so quick, I really didn't have time to prepare myself for it ... But I'm relieved, very relieved."

Brett said the most he wanted out of this game was one hit.

"It's such a shock. I came in here needing four hits and I didn't know if I'd take one swing and my season could be over," he said.

"It happened so fast. It was the farthest thing from my mind to get four hits tonight."

Brett wasted no time after getting three hits, a double and two singles off Julio Valera, in his first three at-bats. He drilled the first pitch from Angels left-hander Tim Fortugno, and Oberkfell had no chance to make a play.

Brett was hugged by Royals first-base coach Lynn Jones and shook hands with Angels first baseman Gary Gaetti. His Royals teammates poured onto the field and swarmed around him. Some players carried cameras.

Then Brett headed toward the dugout, raising his hands to the cheering crowd. He returned to first base followed by a bank of photographers. Then after an out, perhaps distracted by the moment, Brett was picked off first base by Fortugno.

"I was right in the middle of a conversation with Gaetti and he picked me off," Brett said, laughing.

Brett batted a fifth time in the ninth and again reached base, but this time on an error by Oberkfell. He was replaced by a pinch runner, Gary Thurman.

Typically, Brett's hits were significant in the Royals' 4-0 victory. He scored after a first-inning double, and his third-inning single helped score a run in the third. No. 2,999 was a single to center in the fifth.

B rett toasts fellow teammates after getting hit No. 3,000.

by Jo-Ann Barnas

Brett Gets Another 3,000

Of all the congratulatory letters and gifts the Royals' George Brett has received since reaching 3,000 hits six weeks ago, perhaps the most unusual gift came from golfer Fred Couples.

"I sent him 3,000 golf balls last month for all of those hits," Couples said by phone Monday from La Quinta, Calif. "I think he's already gotten them, so his garage should be full."

Couples and Brett, who are golfing buddies, used to live near each other in Palm Springs, Calif. Couples said he recently received a message from Brett to call him—presumably, Couples thinks, to thank him for the golf balls.

How Brett's Four Hits Were Called

October 2, 1992

Here are the play-by-play descriptions of George Brett's four hits the night he reached 3,000.
First inning, Denny Matthews:
"There's a fly ball to short left field, might drop, and it does. The left fielder had a chance to catch it but didn't, and Brett is on his way to second base. Rob Ducey was there and just didn't catch it. They're going to score that a hit. George is three hits shy of 3,000."
Third inning, Fred White:
"Ground ball, headed for right field ... That's a hit, he's two away. 2,998 and two away from 3,000 for George Brett."
Fifth inning, Matthews:
"There's a drive into center field, it's going to drop. Brett is three out of three. The pitch was down, and George just dropped the bat head down at it. So he is at 2,999 and charging."
Seventh inning, White:
"George Brett, from El Segundo, California, will face Tim Fortugno to take his first shot at 3,000. Twenty-one years ago, George Brett left his boyhood home in El Segundo to go to Billings, Mont., to start his professional career, and now here he is, 35 miles from his boyhood home, one hit from 3,000. The pitch ... hot shot at the second baseman, past Oberkfell into right field, Brett's aboard, let's see how they score it ... It was a shot that handcuffed the second baseman.

"He got it. It's a hit. No. 3,000. He almost took the glove off Oberkfell, and his teammates have him surrounded at first. George Brett has done it. "

—Courtesy WDAF (610 AM)

1992

by Jeffrey Flanagan

Brett Says Team Wants Him to Quit

While the Royals announced Friday that they have exercised their option on George Brett's contract for 1993, the message Brett says he's getting privately from the club is different.

And that message isn't one Brett wants to hear.

Brett said by phone from his home Friday that Royals management—he would not verify whom—is urging him to retire.

"Those people I've talked with in the Royals organization said they thought it would be better to open up a roster spot for someone younger and more deserving," Brett said. "They didn't want me back. Younger … and more deserving? That blew me away.

"I thought for someone in my position that was an insult. And the people I've talked to afterward about it were aghast. They thought it was an insult, too.

"It hurt. I just thought it was a strong thing to say. I didn't really know how to react. My jaw hit the floor. I didn't say anything."

Brett, 39, hasn't decided whether he will leave or return to the club for his 20th season in 1993.

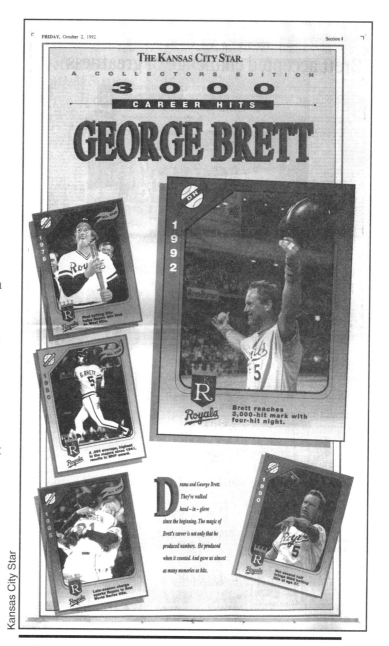

Kansas City Star

After 19 memorable seasons with the Royals, Brett was stunned by comments made by Royals management urging him to retire.

november 3, 1992

by Jeffrey Flanagan

Kauffman Apologizes to Brett

A potential feud brewing between George Brett and the Royals was defused in a flash Monday when owner Ewing Kauffman offered a public apology to Brett.

Kauffman and the Royals called a news conference Monday morning at Royals Stadium because of what Kauffman termed a misunderstanding between himself and Brett over Brett's baseball future.

Brett said Friday that the Royals were urging him to retire and were hoping to open a spot on the roster for a "younger and more deserving player."

Kauffman opened Monday's news conference with this statement:

"The reason for this meeting is that I wanted to publicly apologize to George Brett and the thousands and thousands of baseball

> ## The reason for this meeting is that I wanted to publicly apologize to George Brett and the thousands and thousands of baseball fans throughout the country who love to see him play.
> ### —Ewing Kauffman

Brett, who is considering retirement, was in Arizona and could not be reached for comment Monday.

The issue unfolded last week after the Royals exercised their option on Brett's contract for 1993.

fans throughout the country who love to see him play.

"I have given George the wrong impression in a discussion I had with him in my home and I would like to state without any equivocation whatsoever that the Royals want George Brett to play."

1992

november 12, 1992

by Dick Kaegel

Brett Is a Hit at Party

George Brett made another hit Wednesday night, at least with those who helped him raise funds to find the cause and cure for ALS.

Brett was the smiling centerpiece of a reception given at Halls Crown Center to thank contributors to the fight against amyotrophic lateral sclerosis, better known as Lou Gehrig's disease.

The Royals' star made his quest for 3,000 hits this season a way to raise money for ALS, a project in which he has been involved since 1976. The balls he struck for hits 2,975 to 2,998 were auctioned off. In addition, 20 corporations and individuals each donated $3,000 to the project.

Bob Bjorseth, president of the local ALS chapter, said Brett's chase of 3,000 hits inspired $127,000 in contributions.

"It was a very singular thing that George made into something that benefited others," Bjorseth said. "To my knowledge, it's never been done before. That's what sets George aside."

Brett became involved in the ALS drive after a friend, Keith Worthington, became afflicted with the ailment. Worthington, a clothing-store executive, worked to fight ALS until his death in 1984.

"I saw what ALS did to him," Brett told the gathering at Halls. "I saw him go from a cane to crutches to a wheelchair to a respirator and it finally took his life ... He knew they'd never find a cure for this disease in

Staff photo, Kansas City Star

Sue Worthington, widow of Keith Worthington, with George Brett.

time to save his life but, until the day he died, he tried to make other patients feel more comfortable and to maybe find a cure down the road."

Contributors were given an autographed water color rendition of Brett's 3,000th hit taken from photographs by Joe Ledford of *The Kansas City Star*. Fifty were prepared by Strauss-Peyton, Inc.

Brett gave no hint about whether he would retire or continue playing. In fact, he indicated a decision may be a while in coming.

december 19, 1992

by **Tom** Jackman

Brett's Sticky Homer Gets Its Day in 'Court'

A Mock Trial for the Hometown Bar Association Upholds American League Ruling on the Pine Tar Hit

The verdict: George Brett was not guilty.

The sentence, nevertheless: Life.

The case: Brett's famous "pine tar" home run.

The trial was conducted Friday by an impatient U.S. District Judge Scott O. Wright, who was hurrying to get to his tennis game.

Defense lawyer Paul Vardeman paced the courtroom in a Royals jersey and hat.

Plaintiffs' lawyer Timothy O'Leary wore a New York Yankees ensemble. Wright donned a Royals hat to go with his "Maximum Scott" T-shirt and bright green shorts.

"Let's get on with this," Wright commanded. "I've got a tennis game."

Vardeman called Brett to the stand, even though plaintiffs usually call witnesses first.

O'Leary objected, but Wright overruled.

"Anything to move this case along is OK by me," the judge said.

Brett took the stand, stated his name and his profession. When Vardeman asked whether Brett was employed, Brett said, "At this time, no. But hopefully, someday."

Brett has not decided whether to return for a 20th season with the Royals. Brett has said the Royals hinted that they would like to see him retire, but the Royals have since said they would welcome Brett's return.

Brett admitted he had more than 18 inches of pine tar on his bat when he yanked Goose Gossage's fastball into the Yankee Stadium bleachers. But Brett testified that Yankee manager Billy Martin knew this in the first inning, but waited until the ninth inning to point it out.

"Oh," O'Leary said, "and I suppose that's what you told the umpire and crew, Mr. Brett, when you charged out onto the field screaming like a madman?"

Brett responded: "Of course that's what I said. Look at the replay. You could read my lips. I said, 'With due respect, I take issue with your decision. Let's have lunch tomorrow and discuss it.'"

O'Leary played the videotape of Brett storming the field, being restrained by teammates as he shouted at the umpires.

O'Leary turned and asked, "What about that, Mr. Brett?"

Brett smiled and said, "That's my story. I'm sticking to it."

The crowd roared. The audience of more than 500 lawyers was the largest ever for the annual bar meeting.

Turning to Brett, Wright said, "I will place George Brett on probation with the condition that he remain in Kansas City and play for the Royals for the rest of his life."

And with that, Wright dismissed the Yankees' appeal.

1992

Talis Bergmanis, Kansas City Star

George Brett appeared relaxed during a mock trial at the Kansas City Metropolitan Bar Association's annual meeting. U.S. District Judge Scott O. Wright (left) presided and Paul Vardeman defended Brett in the case of the "pine tar" home run.

He was clearly one of the best players of his generation, but he had a style that spanned generations. He looked and carried himself like a baseball player and could have been at home in any era.
—Bob Costas on George Brett

18

1993

The End of the Line

Early in the year, George Brett made the announcement that he would be back to play for one more year. And what a year it would be. Brett became a father in March when his first son, Jackson Richard, was born.

Soon after, Brett told the press that he planned to retire at the end of the season. "Maybe it's 20 years of playing and maybe it's being a father for the first time, a newlywed still, I guess," Brett said.

After admitting that he had lost his drive, Brett had a strong season, and his teammates and fans knew he was capable of playing another year. But Brett wanted to go out on top, and for him, this was the right time.

His last game at Kauffman Stadium was an emotional one, filled with cheers and tears. A trip around the stadium to salute his fans ended with Brett hopping off and kissing home plate.

On Oct. 3 at Arlington Stadium in Texas, George Brett took his final at-bat as a Royal. He bounced a single up the middle and fittingly ended his glorious career by saluting the crowd after his 3,154th hit.

by Jeffrey Flanagan

He'll Play

Brett Decides to Come Back, Will Be with Royals in 1993

George Brett is coming back.

Brett told *The Kansas City Star* on Wednesday he will return for his 20th season with the Royals in 1993, and he will announce those intentions at a news conference today.

Brett, who reached the 3,000-hit plateau last September, said he has not yet spoken to General Manager Herk Robinson or owner Ewing Kauffman about his decision.

Brett, 39, had been contemplating his decision to return or retire since the season ended in October.

He conferred with several present and former players, including Hall of Fame catcher Johnny Bench and former Royals pitcher Dan Quisenberry, during this off-season but said his decision to return was influenced more by the positive reaction he received from fans.

"It was kind of strange, but every time I went through an airport or went somewhere, I had people telling me, 'Hey, come back one more year. It wouldn't be the same without you,'" Brett said by phone from his home. "Hearing those kind of things really made me feel like coming back.

"I had talked to a lot of people, and probably only about two or three said this would be a good time to cut it off. The rest just kind of said, 'Hey, if you feel you can play, then play.'"

Brett said his wife, Leslie, also encouraged him to return.

"Oh yeah, she said to go for it," Brett said. "She knew that's what I wanted to do anyway."

Brett talked to Manager Hal McRae shortly before Christmas and said McRae also gave a thumbs-up to his return.

"He told me I would hit third and DH and play every day," Brett said.

Brett has not spoken with Kauffman since the two had a discussion at Kauffman's home in November. At that meeting, Kauffman urged Brett to retire, enabling the Royals to open a spot on the roster for, Kauffman said, a "younger, more deserving player."

After that meeting was revealed in a story in *The Kansas City Star*, Kauffman and the Royals held a news conference at which Kauffman offered a public apology to Brett.

Kauffman, though, has yet to offer the apology in person or by phone to Brett.

Brett said he is eager to begin the 1993 season and began preparations for spring training by working out Wednesday at Royals Stadium.

Brett's spring-training schedule will be interrupted around March 12, which is when Leslie's baby is due.

march 8, 1993

by The Kansas City Star

Bretts Are Parents

BASEBALL CITY, Fla.—Oh baby! It's a boy. Kansas City's most anticipated birth of the year took place Monday morning at 7:20 when Leslie Brett delivered Jackson Richard at St. Luke's Hospital.

Jackson Richard Brett, 8 pounds, 9 ounces, is 20 ½ inches long and has thick, dark hair.

Father George and Leslie, and their firstborn, are resting comfortably.

"It was unbelievable," George said by phone from the hospital. "The most amazing thing was first seeing it, and knowing you have a baby, and then seeing it after a shampoo and everything. Then it all hits you. It's a baby."

Tammy Ljungblad, Kansas City Star

George Brett and his wife, Leslie, introduce Jackson Brett.

1993

by Dick Kaegel

Brett's Approach to Hitting Changes with the Times

BASEBALL CITY, Fla.—There's an overhauled George Brett heading your way for the 1993 season.

The old model hit .285 last year, good enough to tie for the Royals' club lead and good enough to make an ordinary player happy.

George Brett, of course, is not your ordinary player.

Brett has a .307 career average and that's more of what he has in mind this year. That, and more power and more run production.

To do that, Brett is making changes.

"It's like I'm learning to hit all over again," he said. "I have to."

Brett is making concessions to age. He'll be 40 years old May 15, early in his 20th season with the Royals.

And this spring training has been different than recent camps for him. He's gone back to being a student of batting.

"It's been a great spring because I'm working on something," he said. "Every day, I work on something. Usually in spring training, I'd come here and swing and really not know

Steve Gonzales, Kansas City Star

In his 20th season with the Royals, George Brett is adjusting his approach to hitting by getting back to the fundamentals.

what I was working on.

"But this year, I'm working on something—every at-bat, every swing in batting practice, every time I go to the cage and take a hundred swings. Rather than just working to get comfortable, I'm working on my fundamentals."

The reason is simple.

"Because I hit .285 last year and I'll be 40 years old," he said. "I have to have my bat ready to hit a little earlier. So we're exaggerating that now in batting practice so I can get the feel for it and then, hopefully, when the season starts I can go back to hitting normally but the fundamentals will stay the way they are now."

Brett's power has fallen off since he hit 24 homers in 1988, his last 100-plus RBI year. In each of the last two years, he's had 61 RBIs with 10 and then seven homers.

1993

Brett Losing the Fire

BALTIMORE—For George Brett, this is it. Probably.

Brett, in his 20th year with the Royals, said Sunday that he plans to retire as a player after this season.

"As of right now, I really don't see myself playing next year," he said.

Brett, though, quickly allowed room for a change of heart.

"I'm not coming out and etching it in stone," he said. "I'm writing it on paper with a No. 2 pencil right now—just real light on a piece of paper: 'This is probably my last year.'

"You know, you can always get out the chisel and the hammer and go down to the sidewalk, knock out the 'probably' and say, 'This is my last year.'"

The remark came up casually during a pregame conversation about Brett's sluggish April and Manager Hal McRae's plan to platoon Brett with Keith Miller in the designated-hitter spot.

"The game is still fun but not as much fun," Brett said. "It seems like I really don't get that disappointed in my performance when I do something bad and, when I do something good, I don't get that excited. So there's something missing somewhere in there.

"Don't get me wrong. I still go out and try to get a hit every time up and I still run balls out and do whatever I can do to help this team win ballgames. But … it's hard to explain."

Last winter Brett wrestled with the retirement question. He had achieved his 3,000th hit and had become a husband to Leslie and a father to Jackson Richard. Ultimately, he decided to return.

At the time, he said a good season might prompt him to come back in 1994 and beyond, even with another club as a free agent.

However, on Sunday, he said, "As of right now, if I had to make the decision today, regardless of what happens this year—even if I had a great year—I wouldn't come back."

And the thought of donning anything but Royal blue apparently has evaporated.

"Can you imagine Michael Jordan playing with anybody but the Bulls?" he said.

"I don't know what it is. Maybe it's 20 years of playing and maybe it's being a father for the first time, a newlywed still, I guess. Baseball before, when I was single all those years, was always the most important thing in my life. That's all I had. Now I have more."

Brett will be 40 on May 15. His career has been glorious, one that will surely put him in the Hall of Fame.

But now, Brett feels, it may be about time to say goodbye.

"It's like that 'Rocky' movie," Brett said, "when Apollo is his manager and they went into the ghetto to work out and Apollo said he'd lost the eye of the tiger. He said, 'Boy, when I fought you, you had the eye of the tiger, Rock.'

"I've just kind of lost that."

1993

september 26, 1993

by Jeffrey Flanagan

Now Retiring: No. 5, Brett

George Brett had been there before, about a year ago, standing solemnly at the intersection of baseball and the rest of his life.

This time, Brett, who led the Royals to six division titles and their only World Series championship in 1985, chose the path away from playing baseball, the endeavor that forever changed his identity.

Brett, 40, announced Saturday his plans to retire from baseball at the end of this season, his 21st with the Royals, at a news conference at Kauffman Stadium.

Brett, who said he began leaning toward retirement shortly after the All-Star break in July, will play his final home game Wednesday night, and his final game next Sunday in Texas. Then he will move immediately into the club's front office as Royals vice president of baseball operations.

As vice president, a position promised under the lifetime contract he signed in 1984 with the Royals and then co-owner Avron Fogelman, Brett will have a broad range of duties, from consulting with key sponsors to evaluating Royals' players and personnel.

Brett, who is one of 19 players in baseball history with more than 3,000 hits, announced his retirement with a cracking voice and moistening eyes:

"After five days of some serious soul-searching, I have decided to retire. I always said I would not play the game for money. And I think my decision is proof of that.

"I've accomplished more in my playing days than I thought I ever would. I've played more games, gotten more hits, more home runs, played in more championship series, more All-Star Games and injured my knee more times than I ever thought I would.

"The one thing that I'm proud of most, and I say this sincerely, is spending my whole career with one team. I will always have respect for this organization ….

"My baseball career is not ending. It's just taking a different direction."

Brett was flanked at the news conference by his wife, Leslie; son, Jackson; Muriel Kauffman, the widow of late owner Ewing Kauffman; and Royals General Manager Herk Robinson.

After Brett read his statement, Kauffman turned to him and said, "I love you dearly. We appreciate the way you have helped us be the best expansion team in the history of baseball.

"You even played when you were hurt, and sometimes I didn't approve of that because you were a special commodity that we wanted to keep well and healthy."

She also cited her husband's biggest thrill, when Brett hit a three-run home run off Goose Gossage that gave the Royals a three-game sweep over the Yankees in the 1980 playoffs.

Reaction from players and coaches was similar in tribute.

"He's just very special," Royals coach Jamie Quirk, Brett's longtime friend, said through tears.

Robinson said: "The way he has gone about everything he has done in his career has meant more to the Kansas City Royals than anything possibly could."

Brett first will be eligible for election to the Hall of Fame in 1999, after he has been retired for five seasons.

Yet walking away from his playing career was not as trying as Brett had expected it to be.

"When I had a meeting with my brother Bobby and my agent (Dennis Gilbert) in Oakland on Monday," Brett said, "Bobby asked me how much it would take for me to play again. I said, 'At this time, they don't have enough money.' I had my mind made up."

Brett knew he had begun to lose his passion for the game this season.

"The game became a job," he said. "It wasn't a game anymore. And baseball shouldn't be treated that way.

"I wasn't getting that excited when I did something good, wasn't getting that down when I did something bad. I wasn't that happy when we won; I wasn't that sad when we lost. There's something missing.

"The only thing I can equate it to is if you ride the same roller coaster for 162 times, 20 years in a row, don't you want to go on another ride once in a while? I want to go on Space Mountain, Mr. Toad's Wild Ride. I'm tired.

"I think the game just beat me, which, it beats everybody in time. It beat Nolan Ryan. It took 26 years to beat Nolan. Well, it took 20 to beat me."

Brett's favorite moment?

"Probably hugging Bret Saberhagen on the mound in 1985," he said. "Winning the World Series."

Worst moment?

"Today," he said. "Right now."

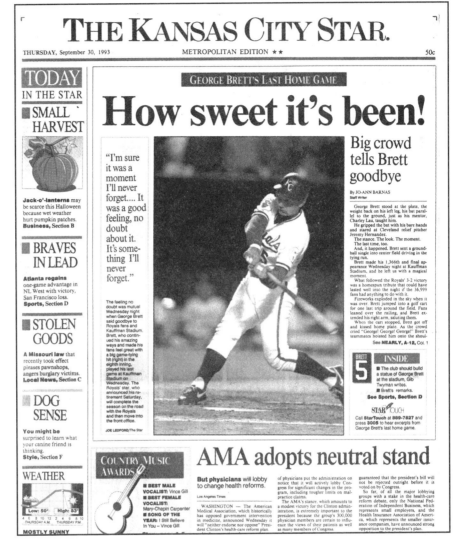

THE KANSAS CITY STAR.

THURSDAY, September 30, 1993   METROPOLITAN EDITION ★★   50¢

GEORGE BRETT'S LAST HOME GAME

How sweet it's been!

"I'm sure it was a moment I'll never forget.... It was a good feeling, no doubt about it. It's something I'll never forget."

Big crowd tells Brett goodbye

By JO-ANN BARNAS
Staff Writer

AMA adopts neutral stand

by Jo-Ann Barnas

How Sweet It's Been!

1993

George Brett stood at the plate, the weight back on his left leg, his bat parallel to the ground, just as his mentor, Charley Lau, taught him.

He gripped the bat with his bare hands and stared at Cleveland relief pitcher Jeremy Hernandez.

The stance. The look. The moment.

The last time, too.

And, it happened. Brett sent a ground-ball single into center field, driving in the tying run.

Brett made his 1,366th and final appearance Wednesday night at Kauffman Stadium, and he left us with a magical moment.

What followed the Royals' 3-2 victory was a homespun tribute that could have lasted well into the night if the 36,999 fans had anything to do with it.

Fireworks exploded in the sky when it was over. Brett jumped into a golf cart for one last trip around the field. Fans leaned over the railing, and Brett extended his right arm, saluting them.

When the cart stopped, Brett got off and kissed home plate.

As the crowd cried "George! George! George!" Brett's teammates hoisted him onto the shoulders of Mike Macfarlane and Mark Gubicza for one last heartfelt tribute.

No, Brett won't forget Wednesday. Not the cheers. Not the hundreds of flashbulbs that lit up the stadium every time he was in view.

"I'm sure it was a moment I'll never forget," Brett said. "Driving around in the golf cart, the fans' reaction obviously made me feel very warm and very appreciated over the years.

"It was a good feeling, no doubt about it. It's something I'll never forget."

For the fans who were there, it was their one last look, one last time to say goodbye to No. 5.

How to summarize two decades in a moment? How do you capture the full essence of the greatest baseball player ever to pull on a Royals uniform?

The fans did it the only way they knew how. They gave him a standing ovation. Not once, but every time he stepped onto the field.

"He's the whole Kansas City team to us," said teary-eyed Bonnie Maple, 81, a baseball season-ticket holder for 33 years.

"It's happy and sad both. George has just been a part of all of us for so long."

It seemed just as hard to Brett to say goodbye. He said as much last Saturday when he announced his retirement, although he kept stressing he won't really be gone. He'll still be active in his new job as vice president/baseball operations. In fact, he will travel with Herk Robinson to the general manager's meeting in November in Florida.

"I can still play, but not like I once did," Brett said during his pregame news confer-

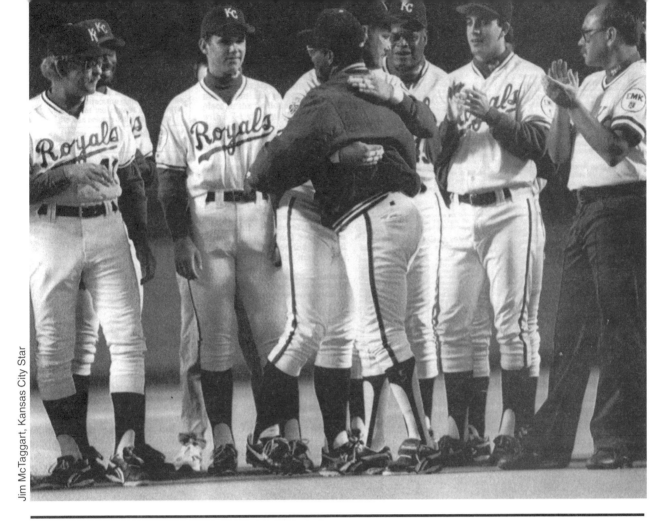

George Brett embraces Hal McRae at the end of pre-game festivities at Kauffman Stadium. Brett received gifts from his teammates.

ence. "The game has become a job to me. The game deserves better."

Brett realized during the summer that greatness alone can't turn back the clock; that when spirit and will can't stretch a single into a double, it's time to move on.

Still, many of his closest friends weren't convinced.

"I would test him as the season went along," said Jamie Quirk, a Royals coach and one of Brett's closest friends. "In Oakland (last Monday) he hit an opposite-field home run. He came back to the dugout and I said, 'You're going to play again, right?'

"He answered, 'No.'

"Even now, it seems strange. Not to see George Brett in a Royals uniform will take some getting used to."

But while Brett was confident of his decision, ending a career in which he has collected 3,153 hits—a sure pass into the Hall of Fame—it didn't make his last drive to Kauffman Stadium any easier. For him. Or his fans.

Brett's day began normal enough. Coffee and the crossword puzzle. A bridge game and d'Bronx deli for lunch.

He left his house at 3:10 p.m., with his older brother John, who along with two other brothers and their mother, Ethel Johnson, came to Kansas City for the final game.

As Brett drove past Mission Hills Country Club on his way to the ballpark, he turned to John and said, "Maybe next year at this time, I'll be there playing golf."

october 4, 1993

by Gib Twyman

Last Hit Paid Tribute to an Unmatched Career

ARLINGTON, Texas—For 21 years, the Lord has given us this day our daily Brett.

Now he has been taken away.

And that, my good friends and neighbors, is it.

Give No. 5 one last high five. You will never see another like him in our town.

Did you get the finality of that word, never? Good.

Every now and then I hear "probably won't" and "maybe not" creep into conversations about Brett. Forget those words. There'll never be another George Brett, period.

This goes far beyond numbers, imposing as they are. Brett will go down as the only man in history with 3,000 hits, 600 doubles, 100 triples, 300 homers and 200 stolen bases. And the only one to win batting titles in three decades (1976, 1980, 1990).

Some day, some kid may come along who strings together some serious years for us. He'll never be another Brett.

The economics work against a guy staying with one team more than a few years, much less 20. And with Ewing Kauffman's industrial-strength deep pockets gone, KC might have trouble holding a franchise player.

But mostly we'll never see another Brett because, uniquely, he had the "whole package" as a superstar. He was great in the game, great with teammates and great with fans and reporters.

With his statistics, Brett easily could have taken on an I-am-the-star attitude. In-stead, he was the first guy to take rookies under his wing.

I know, I know, someone out there undoubtedly got stiffed on an autograph request. But no athlete can honor every request. Brett was diligent about autographs. If he made someone feel bad, then it was leaving the 201st after signing 200. You can't avoid that.

Brett had a couple celebrated run-ins with news media representatives. But on balance, he bent over backward for the press, and he was so quotable he almost couldn't help himself.

"I know I had my bad moments here and there," Brett said. "But when I took that last trip around the (Kauffman) stadium in the golf cart, it was like all was forgotten."

The thing we won't forget is Brett in the big moments. He danced with destiny again Sunday in his last at-bat against Texas.

He'd gone zero-for-11 since getting a hit Wednesday in his last at-bat at Kauffman Stadium. Now, either Brett was going to finish out ohfer-Texas, or he was going to do something to make us remember.

He got a hit.

But the way it happened offers a fascinating insight into the way baseball works and the impression Brett has made on his game the last 21 years.

Tom Henke was out there, a smoke-throwing country boy from rural Missouri, one of the premier relievers in baseball. And

1993

to make matters more interesting, Brett was fighting the biggest case of nerves he'd ever had.

"It was my most emotional at-bat of my life," he said.

At 4:09, he walked to the batter's box. Overcast, 72 degrees, wind slightly toward right. As he dug in, his teammates came as one to the top of the dugout.

"Nothing planned. Totally spontaneous," Jamie Quirk said.

Nolan Ryan came out and offered his cap emphatically at Brett. The Rangers all were at the top step now. Brett didn't see them. Just his guys.

"My eyes were filling up," he said. "I said to myself, 'These guys are really into this last at-bat.' I wanted to do something special. I didn't want to strike out."

Henke had made up his mind to throw Brett nothing but fastballs. No nasty forkballs. He brought high heat the first pitch. High and outside. Ball one. Second pitch, more heat. Brett swung through. Strike one.

It wasn't until then that Henke got his message through: Nothing but fastballs, George.

"He nodded at me. I winked back at him," Henke said.

The next fastball, Brett slung foul. And the next one, he bounced up the middle.

The eyes told you that Manny Lee, the Texas shortstop, could have caught the ball. He broke late to his left and didn't extend well as the ball went past.

Jim McTaggart, Kansas City Star

Brett bats for the final time of his career against the Texas Rangers at Arlington Stadium on October 3, 1993.

Years from now, people may remember that hit as a solid single to center. Even if it's recalled as a catchable bouncer through the box, it won't matter much. Not much at all.

You know what that hit was? It was pure tribute to Brett from the very guys who'd give it most grudgingly—his opponents.

It was their nod, their we-are-not-worthy bow, if you will.

They, like us, knew they'd never see another one like him.

George's accomplishments and contributions during the last 28 years remain everlasting throughout the organization and our community. The Royals organization is proud of the fact that George has been associated with the Royals since the onset of his professional career.

—Herk Robinson, Royals Executive Vice President
and General Manager

For George Brett, the transition from player to spectator was not an easy one. As Kansas City's most revered athlete, Brett began his "retirement" by seeing his jersey retired at Kauffman Stadium along with those of Frank White and Dick Howser. Thousands of fans gathered to see their "No. 5" one last time.

Although he was now retired, Brett could never really get away from "his" game. His new position with the Royals as vice president of baseball operations enabled him to remain close to baseball. He also returned to the batter's box when he participated in the 1998 All-Star Game celebrity hitting contest. Brett cranked two home runs, and it was clear that he was thrilled to be back where he felt most comfortable, on the ball field.

by Jeffrey Flanagan

Brett Sharpens Transition Game

He's Still on Field but Finds Retirement a Good Fit

BASEBALL CITY, Fla.—If you didn't know differently, you'd think nothing had changed for George Brett this spring.

No. 5 comes early to the ballpark each day, and he uses the same locker he has for the seven years the Royals have called Baseball City their spring home.

Brett's morning routine remains fixed: He still sips coffee as he negotiates the daily crossword puzzle and still chats it up with the players before eventually pulling on his Royals uniform. Then it's out to the Stadium Field for the day's workout.

"It almost seems like he's still on the team," right-hander Mark Gubicza said.

But Brett remains on the team in a wistful sense only. After 21 seasons, Brett is no longer in camp as a player, no longer a slave to the daily grind.

Instead, Brett is continuing to feel out the wide-ranging duties of his new position as vice president of baseball operations.

Over the winter, that job description included evaluating player personnel. This spring, Brett is acting as an additional coach, hitting fungos, throwing batting practice and discreetly passing out advice.

"I think the players listen, too, because it's George Brett talking," Manager Hal McRae said.

Brett's present role appears to be a smooth fit for the team and himself. The quite-often bungee jump from active player to retired player has been less traumatic.

"I'm really enjoying it, to be truthful," Brett said. "I have no regrets about retiring. None.

"And the things I'm doing this spring, like throwing BP and hitting fungos, has made the transition easier. I don't feel that I'm missing anything from when I was a player."

Brett is also beginning to slowly edge away from the news media's eyes. Reporters no longer crowd around his locker, though it would be impossible for him to ever fade into anonymity.

"That part has been far more normal this spring," he said. "It's been great. I knew I wouldn't miss that.

"Players have always said that the only thing you really miss after you retire is not the game itself but the other players. It's the camaraderie. I can see that. But I still feel like I'm a part of it, sitting here and talking to the guys."

1994-98

George Brett visits with Oakland A's manager Tony La Russa and the umpires before the start of a game.

George Brett and Royals general manager Herk Robinson watch a game at Kauffman Stadium.

may 15, 1994

by Blair Kerkhoff

You Won't See No. 5 Anymore

His Uniform Joins Brett in Retirement

On this occasion even the few bad memories were erased.

"The good times now are great times," George Brett said. "The bad times are good times."

With that, Brett's No. 5 jersey was retired Saturday by the Royals. In an emotional Kauffman Stadium ceremony delayed an hour by rain, Brett, who turns 41 today, and Kansas City thanked each other for a relationship that has spanned half of Brett's life and most of the Royals' 26 seasons.

"I have been with this organization more than half of my life, and I can honestly say this is the best half of my life," Brett said. "I want to thank you all for making me a Kansas City citizen."

Before the ceremony, in which Brett held his 14-month-old son, Jackson, father and son Brett entered the Royals' dugout with the younger Brett high-fiving his dad's former teammates.

When it was over, father and son climbed into a red Corvette and circled the stadium. They stopped briefly in front of the visitors' dugout, where several of the Oakland Athletics, led by Manager Tony La Russa, extended a hand in congratulations for the player who amassed 3,154 career hits and 317 home runs and played in six championship series and two World Series.

"This is one of the most special moments in Royals history," Royals General Manager Herk Robinson said in introducing Brett. "His extraordinary talents have meant more to this city than words can express."

Royals board of directors member Muriel Kauffman, wife of late club owner Ewing Kauffman, gave Brett a diamond-studded ring with the No. 5 set in stone and his career accomplishments engraved. She gave Brett's wife, Leslie, a matching pendant.

Brett's No. 5 won't be worn again by a Royal, but several in the near-capacity crowd wore variations of the Brett jersey and don't plan to put away theirs.

"This is time for us to pay back to him what he's given us all these years," said Jeff Stubblefield of Manhattan, Kansas, wearing a grey pinstripe No. 5. "If you're a Royals fan you have to be here."

Amy Moutray, a Northwest Missouri State student from Barnard, Mo., got her No. 5 Royals white pinstripe jersey for her 16th birthday. On a visit to Toronto's SkyDome in 1992, she had Brett's name stitched on.

"I've always loved George Brett," Moutray said. "I had to be here for this."

More than four hours before the first

Orlin Wagner, AP/Wide World Photos

George Brett (left), Frank White (center) and Nancy Howser, widow of manager Dick Howser, threw out ceremonial first balls at the Royals' home opener. The uniform numbers of Brett, White and Howser were retired during pre-game ceremonies.

pitch, fans lined up outside the gates that didn't open for another hour. During the rain delay, crowds queued up outside the souvenir stands for a shot at a George Brett jersey retirement shirt.

Under her 1985 World Series jacket, Betty Reichert of Overland Park sported a newspaper front-page reproduction on a sweat shirt of Brett's finale last year. Carrie McQueen and her 7-year-old daughter, Kelsey,

of Riverton, Iowa, were among the many family brigades in Brett garb. Julie Kemper of Cameron, Mo., in Royal blue, was one row behind. Hickman Mills senior Melanie Hutman often wears her No. 5 to school.

Brett's jersey is on display in the Royals Hall of Fame exhibit at Kauffman Stadium. His is the first retired Royals jersey that was worn by a player. In 1987, Manager Dick Howser's No. 10 was retired.

august 5, 1995

by Howard Richman

Brett Bags It

That caddie sure looks familiar.

Yes, that was baseball great George Brett serving as caddie for Larry Ziegler.

Brett was introduced to Ziegler in spring training about 18 years ago. Ziegler, a friend of Royals Manager Whitey Herzog, was coaching third base for a day, and when Brett arrived at the bag he razzed the rookie coach.

"He told me, 'You stink,'" Ziegler said, "and I said, 'You don't look so good at the plate, either.'"

Unfortunately, Ziegler shot 1-over 71, leaving him 8 shots off the lead.

"He did everything a caddie could do," Ziegler said of Brett. "I told him I wished I could've played as well as he caddied."

Brett said Ziegler's bag got heavy toward the end.

"I was fine the first nine," Brett said. "Then on the back nine I started humping down a little bit more. My bag weighs like two pounds. It would've been a lot easier if he had taken the bowling balls out of his."

Brett said if Ziegler had shot 68 or better he'd have come back today.

"I guess I'm fired," Brett said. "But this was fun because I enjoy golf."

Brett, who has a 5 handicap, said he'd never consider trying to make the Senior PGA Tour.

"I have as much a chance beating somebody like Tom Watson as Larry does winning this tournament," Brett said.

Joe Ledford, Kansas City Star

Golfer Larry Ziegler and caddie George Brett share a laugh at the St. Luke's Classic golf tournament in Kansas City.

may 20, 1996

by Marisa Agha

Brett Honored for ALS Service

George Brett was reminded again Sunday that there is life after baseball.

The former Kansas City Royals star was honored Sunday as the 1996 winner of the Circle of Champions, an award presented annually by the Len Dawson Celebrity Classic Golf Tournament. It is given "to an individual who represents courage and perseverance both on and off the field," said Andy Smith, tournament director.

About 400 people attended the silent auction and banquet at the Adam's Mark hotel where Dawson presented the award to Brett.

"George is a great ambassador for Kansas City," said Dawson, who approves the recipient each year. "Aside from his athletic ability and what he accomplished with the Royals, he gives of his time to help those less fortunate."

Specifically, Brett was cited for his work with the ALS Foundation, which helps people with Lou Gehrig's disease.

Brett said it was especially gratifying to be honored for his efforts outside of baseball.

"This is exciting," Brett said. "Any time you get an award for services to a community, it's a pretty good home run."

John Sleezer, Kansas City Star

George Brett plays the sax at a pre-game gala to benefit ALS outside of Kauffman Stadium. Brett was honored as the winner of the Circle of Champions award for his work with the ALS foundation.

1994 - 98

july 7, 1998

by Joe Posnanski

In Batter's Box, Brett Makes Present of Past

DENVER—George Brett dug his left foot into the dirt, twisted it back and forth, and he was home. He's 45 now, an old has-been he calls himself, but here in the batter's box, 40,000 watching and screaming, bat wiggling in his hand, George Brett doesn't get old.

"Wasn't that incredible? " he asked. He hit two home runs Monday in this celebrity hitting contest at Coors Field—one of the many fun little extras that go along with today's All-Star Game in Denver—and Brett's team won the trophy, a small award that looked remarkably like something a kid wins at a spelling bee. Brett carried it around, showed it to everybody.

"Look at this trophy," he screamed. "It's glass. But I won it. I'm 45 years old, and I won a home-run hitting contest at the All-Star Game. Can you believe it? I haven't won a piece of glass in five years. Look at this piece of glass. It's beautiful, isn't it? Look at it."

We looked at it. It was beautiful, sort of. It was beautiful to watch Brett hit again, bat pointed straight back, weight shifting from leg to leg, Brett himself ducked down into that crouch. In batting practice, he hit a home run measured at 430 feet, which ain't bad for an old man. In the hitting contest, he outhit the rookies and the former stars and the celebrities, which included actor Kevin Costner and Denver quarterback John Elway.

And he was center stage again, first time in a long time. He had not come to an All-Star Game since his last as a player, 1988, 10 years before, and he stood around nervously before his time at bat, jabbering with some of the younger players, kicking at the grass.

"I was nervous before every game I ever played," he would say. "As soon as you get in that batter's box, though, you calm down. "

And so, there was Brett in the batter's box Monday, poking the ball the opposite way, yanking the inside pitch into the upper deck, letting bad pitches go by, complaining still that he swung at too many other bad pitches. Brett hates when he swings at bad pitches.

"I could have hit another home run if I had waited for my pitch," he said.

"I was shocked at how much it meant to me. I felt that old adrenaline. I felt those juices pumping. Can you believe that?"

Brett should have known. Every time he steps into the box, it becomes a religious experience. Last year, he took batting practice at Coors Field, and he whacked the ball all over the place, hit a bunch of home runs, and he was seriously, realistically and absolutely contemplating a comeback. Oh, maybe the feeling left him as soon as he walked away, but in that box, he felt young again. He always does.

"That was so much fun," he said Monday after hitting his home runs and his line drives, after swinging the bat and hearing the crowd again. Brett sounded like a little kid. "I mean, that was so great. Wow. That was such a blast."

George Brett could not have been happier when he won the home-run-hitting contest during the All-Star Game festivities at Coors Field in Denver.

He was giddy and thrilled, and he clung to his small trophy, and he told more stories. People asked him about the pine-tar incident ("I laugh about it," he said) and about trying to hit .400 ("Tony Gwynn's the guy, but he's running out of time.") and about the Hall of Fame ("I hope I did enough, but I don't know."), but Brett really wanted to talk about how he was stroking the ball out there. Felt good. Looked good. He wants to defend his trophy at next year's All-Star Game. He can hit even better, he says, if he can just lay off the bad pitches.

Everyone who has ever played this game, from Little League on up, has a dream. And that dream is to someday make it to the Hall of Fame.

—George Brett

From KC to Cooperstown

"I wish everybody in this room could feel as good as I do right now. It's so special." George Brett said that Tuesday, Jan. 5, 1999, the day he was elected into baseball immortality, the day it was learned he'd be enshrined in sports' most revered hall, the National Baseball Hall of Fame.

Brett wanted us to feel what he was feeling. How ironic. Kansas Citians have long wanted Brett to feel what they were feeling about him, especially on the nights he'd crack a game-winning hit for the Royals or joined the 3,000-hit club or led the Royals to a World Series title. For more than two decades, George Brett has made Kansas Citians feel special, feel good, feel proud.

Tuesday was just more gravy. It was a day to reflect on what George has meant to this city since 1973, the year he broke into the major leagues as a long-haired rookie third baseman. George Brett made Kansas Citians believe in miracles. He made you believe that anything was possible, if you just tried harder than the other guy. He made you believe no obstacle was too great.

Jason Whitlock,
The Kansas City Star Sports Columnist
January 5, 1999

january 5, 1999

by Jeffrey Flanagan

The Call Goes Brett's Way: He's in the Hall of Fame

Yes, the phone call came Tuesday. And yes, George Howard Brett became the first player to be elected into the Baseball Hall of Fame for his achievements as a Kansas City Royal.

But before and after the phone call, Brett seemed to spend the day caught in a perpetual rundown between every human emotion imaginable—between anticipation and uneasiness, euphoria and sadness, humility and gratitude.

Indeed, all in one day, Brett touched every base of his baseball career, from the day he was first scouted by the Royals to the team's World Series title in 1985 and ultimately to his unforgettable final home game when he knelt down and kissed home plate at Kauffman Stadium.

And along the way, he stopped every so often, making sure to thank all the names and faces that made the day possible.

"I just wish every person out there could feel for one minute the way I do today. I really do," a teary-eyed Brett told a huge gathering of reporters, family, friends, former teammates and Kansas City notables at Kauffman Stadium. "It's just very, very special."

Yet well before the afternoon news conference, Brett survived an unexpected dose of anxiety.

The phone call from the Baseball Writers' Association of America, which Brett and his wife, Leslie, thought would come at 11 a.m. didn't come promptly. Not by a long shot.

While Brett sat waiting in the den of his home, the passing minutes seemed like hours.

Even his host of friends and supporters, there to share in the celebration, began to fidget as 11:15 turned into 11:30, then to 11:45 and then to noon.

One friend tapped his fingers on his knees, staring at the three silver-plated bats mounted in one trophy case, the rewards and symbols of Brett's three American League batting titles.

Another friend nervously spun a globe positioned near Brett's desk, while yet another stared blankly at his clasped hands.

Outside the den, Leslie paced the front hallway, her heels click-clicking on the marble.

Later, out of the silence came a soft voice as George and Leslie's 5-year-old son, Jackson, wandered into the den and asked innocently, "Daddy, Daddy. Did you get the phone call yet?"

"Not yet. Soon, I hope. Soon," George answered with a faint smile.

Not that the phone didn't ring. Four times it did, in fact, and all four were false alarms. Just more friends wanting to know the scoop.

At 12:15, George looked up at long-time buddy Ed Molotsky and cracked: "Aw, hell, Ed. I guess I should have played one more year."

Molotsky chuckled and replied, "Guess so."

1999

Mercifully, at 12:20, another ring. The real deal?

"Hello?" George answered.

"George, this is Jack O'Connell from the Baseball Writers' Association.

"Congratulations."

A huge smile of relief finally crossed Brett's face and as he turned to the rest of the room, he offered a big thumbs-up.

"We all just kind of dropped our shoulders and sighed in relief," Molotsky said. "Whew."

Added Leslie: "I was going crazy. I couldn't pace anymore after awhile and I went and did some laundry. Everyone was just so relieved for George when he finally got the call."

The reason for the delay was more of a misunderstanding than anything. The writers' association suggests it will call during an 11 a.m.-1 p.m. window on the day of the announcement.

Robin Yount, elected along with Nolan Ryan and Brett, was the first to get his call. And that was fine with Brett, who has long considered Yount one of his closest friends.

"I had more fun playing against Robin than any other player during my career," said Brett, his eyes tearing up for one of many encores during the day. "So when Jack told me he'd already called Robin to congratulate him, that's when I lost it. I just lost it."

After the phone call, Brett and crew hugged, laughed and made their way slowly to the kitchen for lunch.

"Pizza," Molotsky said, "best thing to relieve tension."

By 1 p.m., Brett was on the phone again, addressing baseball writers from around the country on a conference call. Then as Leslie packed for today's events in New York (another news conference and an appearance with David Letterman), George finished the call, quickly showered and dressed, and the

Julie Jacobson, Kansas City Star

George Brett is greeted by reporters as he arrives for his Hall of Fame selection press conference at Kauffman Stadium.

two hopped in a limousine and headed for Kauffman Stadium.

By 2:30, the fourth floor of the Stadium Club was brimming with reporters, team officials, celebrities and seemingly every person in Kansas City, all there hoping to catch a moment of history.

The Bretts arrived to a standing ovation, bringing yet another round of tears from George.

Then came the presentations. Brett's closest former teammate and friend, Jamie Quirk, introduced him. But the challenge of presenting Brett almost got the best of Quirk, who stopped and restarted often.

At one point, Quirk, virtually sobbing, turned to Brett and said: "I said 'No crying,' remember? Not going to do it."

Later, as Brett prepared to address the gathering, he folded his lips, fighting his own emotions, and peered straight ahead.

"Everyone who has ever played this game," he started, voice shaking, "from Little League on up, has a dream. And that dream is to someday make it to the Hall of Fame ...."

"And that's what makes this so special."

january 5, 1999

by Dick Kaegel

Brett Easily Makes the Hall of Fame

George Brett, who fretted about being elected to the Baseball Hall of Fame, really didn't have to worry.

Brett, the most fabled player in Royals history, was swept into the Cooperstown, N.Y., hall on Tuesday by one of the biggest margins in history.

Nolan Ryan and Brett each were named on more than 98 percent of the record 497 votes cast by the Baseball Writers' Association of America. Robin Yount also was chosen with 77 percent of the vote, just over the required 75 percent.

All three players were chosen in their first year of eligibility, making this the biggest freshman class since the inaugural 1936 group of Ty Cobb, Walter Johnson, Christy Mathewson, Babe Ruth and Honus Wagner.

Brett's Hall of Fame credentials included 3,154 hits, a .305 career average, 317 home runs and three batting titles in his 21 years with the Royals.

The three players will be inducted July 25 in Cooperstown. They bring the total membership to 240, pending the veterans' committee vote in March.

Ryan led the balloting with 491 votes, just three more than Brett's 488. Yount received 385. A total of 373 was necessary to be elected.

"When I was told that I got in and got 98 percent, I was just flabbergasted," Brett said. "It just knocked me on the floor."

The surge of Brett votes ranked him fourth in all-time voting. His 98.19 percent was just behind Tom Seaver's 98.84, Ryan's 98.79 and Ty Cobb's 98.23.

"You think it was the Christmas cards my wife sent out to the voters?" Brett joked at a news conference.

Another first-time candidate, Carlton Fisk, finished fourth in the voting with 330 and failed to reach the Hall. Fisk was followed by Tony Perez, who was runner-up last year, with 302. Dale Murphy, another highly touted first-timer, received just 96 votes.

Minnie Minoso and Mickey Lolich were also-rans for the 15th year and will go off the ballot.

Brett received a higher percentage of the vote than Babe Ruth, Hank Aaron, Willie Mays, Stan Musial, Ted Williams, Joe DiMaggio and other great hitters of the past.

He became the first player elected for his accomplishments with the Royals.

"George was the Kansas City Royals," former teammate Jamie Quirk said Tuesday at the Stadium Club.

"We had some great players. A lot of them are in this room today, but George was our heart and soul."

Brett recalled that he was disappointed when the Royals drafted him in 1971. But his brother, Bobby, reminded him that his chances of moving up to the majors were better because the Royals were an expansion team.

"He was right," Brett said.

For 21 years, starting in 1973, he began carving a legendary career that will be commemorated on a plaque in Cooperstown. He flirted with .400 in 1980, played on the 1985 World Series champions and created memories with a crucial home run off Goose Gossage in the 1980 playoffs and one with a pine-tarred bat in 1983.

On a phone conference with BBWAA writers from across the country, Brett was asked about the Pine-Tar Game in New York.

"At the time it wasn't funny," Brett said. "But now my oldest son, Jackson, says, 'Dad, let's put in that tape where you go berserk.' So we fast-forward to that point in the tape and I have to explain to him that's not the type of behavior I expect from him."

Julie Jacobson, Kansas City Star

Brett's youngest son Robin gives his father a "thumbs up" while sitting on his mother Leslie's lap at the press conference.

Third Basemen in the Hall

	G	AB	R	H	2B	3B	HR	RBI	SB	AVG	SLG
Frank Baker	1575	5984	887	1838	315	103	96	987	235	.307	.442
George Brett	**2707**	**10,394**	**1583**	**3154**	**665**	**137**	**317**	**1595**	**201**	**.305**	**.487**
Jimmy Collins	1726	6796	1055	2000	353	116	65	983	194	.294	.409
George Kell	1795	6702	881	2054	385	50	78	870	51	.306	.414
Fred Lindstrom	1438	5611	895	1747	301	81	103	779	84	.311	.449
Eddie Mathews	2391	8537	1509	2315	354	72	512	1453	68	.271	.509
Brooks Robinson	2896	10,654	1232	2848	482	68	268	1357	28	.267	.401
Mike Schmidt	2404	8352	1506	2234	408	59	548	1595	92	.267	.527
Pie Traynor	1941	7559	1183	2416	371	164	58	1273	158	.320	.453

january 5, 1999

by Joe Posnanski

Brett in a Word: Indescribable

George Brett's greatness is too large to condense, too gigantic to abbreviate. You can't boil down all those hits and the batting titles and the moments and the chase for .400 and the pine-tar home run and the way he tormented the Yankees and the thousand times he broke up the double play and the million throws he made across the diamond. George Brett was elected to Baseball's Hall of Fame on Tuesday. You can't capture his brilliance in a few words.

But maybe you can tell a little bit of the story by remembering just one night—October 12, 1985—a Friday night at Royals Stadium. More than 40,000 people were there that night, though there wasn't much hope twirling about. The fountains swooshed listlessly. The Royals had lost two straight playoff games to the Toronto Blue Jays. They had lost 10 straight playoff games over the years. This story has been told over and over again in Kansas City.

"It's OK," Brett told his teammates before the game that Friday. "I'll carry you on my back."

Baseball is not a game built for one man to pull along an entire team. In hockey, a hot goaltender can lug his team to a championship by stopping every puck, and a great quarterback can will his team to victory in football. Michael Jordan knows he will get the last shot at the end of the game, and he knows he will make it.

But baseball is different, it's a subtle game: The surest way not to hit a home run is to go up there and try for one. The most dominant pitcher of our time—Brett's Hall of Fame classmate Nolan Ryan—lost almost as many games as he won. Even the greatest players who ever lived cannot just decide, "OK, today I will hit home runs and make some great plays and carry my team to victory."

Only, that's exactly what George Brett did that night. There was always something different about Brett, something indescribable that opened up inside him when the pressure heightened, when the spotlight shined, when America's eyes glared on him.

I always felt he was the prototypical baseball player. He was as fierce a competitor as I've ever seen. If there was a player I'd ever want to be like, it'd be George Brett.

—Fellow Hall of Famer Robin Yount

Joe Ledford, Kansas City Star

Brett on Baseball's All-Time Lists

GAMES

1. Pete Rose — 3,562
2. Carl Yastrzemski — 3,308
3. Hank Aaron — 3,298
4. Ty Cobb — 3,034
5. Stan Musial — 3,020
6. Willie Mays — 2,992
7. Rusty Staub — 2,951
8. Brooks Robinson — 2,896
9. Robin Yount — 2,855
10. Dave Winfield — 2,850
19. **George Brett** — **2,707**

AT-BATS

1. Pete Rose — 14,053
2. Hank Aaron — 12,364
3. Carl Yastrzemski — 11,988
4. Ty Cobb — 11,429
5. Robin Young — 11,008
11. **George Brett** — **10,349**

RBIs

1. Hank Aaron — 2,297
2. Babe Ruth — 2,211
3. Lou Gehrig — 1,990
4. Ty Cobb — 1,961
5. Stan Musial — 1,951
6. Jimmie Foxx — 1,921
7. Willie Mays — 1,903
8. Mel Ott — 1,860
9. Carl Yastrzemski — 1,844
10. Ted Williams — 1,839
22. **George Brett** — **1,595**
    Mike Schmidt — 1,595

EXTRA-BASE HITS

1. Hank Aaron — 1,477
2. Stan Musial — 1,377
3. Babe Ruth — 1,356
4. Willie Mays — 1,323
5. Lou Gehrig — 1,190
6. Frank Robinson — 1,186
7. Carl Yastrzemski — 1,157
8. Ty Cobb — 1,139
9. Tris Speaker — 1,133
10. **George Brett** — **1,119**

HITS

1. Pete Rose — 4,256
2. Ty Cobb — 4,191
3. Hank Aaron — 3,771
4. Stan Musial — 3,630
5. Tris Speaker — 3,515
6. Honus Wagner — 3,430
7. Carl Yastrzemski — 3,419
8. Eddie Collins — 3,309
9. Willie Mays — 3,283
10. Nap Lajoie — 3,251
11. **George Brett** — **3,154**
12. Paul Waner — 3,152
13. Robin Yount — 3,142
14. Rod Carew — 3,053
15. Cap Anson — 3,041
16. Lou Brock — 3,023
17. Dave Winfield — 3,014
18. Al Kaline — 3,007
19. Roberto Clemente — 3,000

TOTAL BASES

1. Hank Aaron — 6,856
2. Stan Musial — 6,134
3. Willie Mays — 6,066
4. Ty Cobb — 5,863
5. Babe Ruth — 5,793
18. **George Brett** — **5,044**

HOME RUNS

1. Hank Aaron — 755
2. Babe Ruth — 714
3. Willie Mays — 660
4. Frank Robinson — 586
5. Harmon Killebrew — 573
59. **George Brett** — **317**

DOUBLES

1. Tris Speaker — 793
2. Pete Rose — 746
3. Stan Musial — 725
4. Ty Cobb — 724
5. **George Brett** — **665**

Brett's Career

Regular Season

Yr	G	AB	R	H	2B	3B	HR	RBI	AVG
1973	13	40	2	5	2	0	0	0	.125
1974	133	457	49	129	21	5	2	47	.282
1975	159	634	84	195	35	13	11	89	.308
1976	159	645	94	215	34	14	7	67	.333
1977	139	564	105	176	32	13	22	88	.312
1978	128	510	79	150	45	8	9	62	.294
1979	154	645	119	212	42	20	23	107	.329
1980	117	449	87	175	33	9	24	118	.390
1981	89	347	42	109	27	7	6	43	.314
1982	144	552	101	166	32	9	21	82	.301
1983	123	464	90	144	38	2	25	93	.310
1984	104	377	42	107	21	3	13	69	.284
1985	155	550	108	184	38	5	30	112	.335
1986	124	441	70	128	28	4	16	73	.290
1987	115	427	71	124	18	2	22	78	.290
1988	154	589	90	180	42	3	24	103	.306
1989	124	457	67	129	26	3	12	80	.282
1990	142	544	82	179	45	7	14	87	.329
1991	131	505	77	129	40	2	10	61	.255
1992	152	592	55	169	35	5	7	61	.285
1993	145	560	69	149	31	3	19	75	.266
Totals	**2707**	**10349**	**1583**	**3154**	**665**	**137**	**317**	**1595**	**.305**

Division Series

	G	AB	R	H	2B	3B	HR	RBI	AVG
1981	3	12	0	2	0	0	0	0	.167

League Championship Series

	G	AB	R	H	2B	3B	HR	RBI	AVG
1976	5	18	4	8	1	1	1	5	.444
1977	5	20	2	6	0	2	0	0	.300
1978	4	18	7	7	1	1	3	3	.389
1980	3	11	3	3	1	0	2	4	.273
1984	3	13	0	3	0	0	0	0	.231
1985	7	23	6	8	2	0	3	5	.348
Total	**27**	**103**	**22**	**35**	**5**	**4**	**9**	**19**	**.340**

World Series

	G	AB	R	H	2B	3B	HR	RBI	AVG
1980	6	24	3	9	2	1	1	3	.375
1985	7	27	5	10	1	0	0	1	.370
Total	**13**	**51**	**8**	**19**	**3**	**1**	**1**	**4**	**.373**